# MAKING
# SCIENTIFIC
# TOYS

# MAKING
# SCIENTIFIC
# TOYS *by Carson I. A. Ritchie*

THOMAS NELSON, INC., PUBLISHERS
Nashville          New York

*First edition*

Library of Congress Cataloging in Publication Data

Ritchie, Carson I A
    Making scientific toys.

    Includes index.
    1. Toys.  2. Scientific apparatus and instruments.  I. Title.
Q164.R57     688.7'25     75-23110
ISBN 0-8407-6433-2

# CONTENTS

# 1. Tools and Equipment

## Some Words on Making the Toys

Perhaps the words "scientific toys" make you picture elaborate pieces of equipment, expensive materials, and colossal bills. Even when "scientific toys," or demonstration models, are made for laboratories and colleges, that picture does not necessarily apply, however. Often laboratory assistants have to improvise with odds and ends from the laboratory's store cupboard. That is the approach I suggest you use when making the toys in this book. The toys were selected partly because they could be made inexpensively. You may have to buy some supplies, such as the chemicals for the chemical toys, but many of the materials, such as aluminum foil, you will be able to find around the house.

Also, most of the toys are not difficult to make, although the amount of work required does vary from toy to toy. Some complicated toys, such as the sand machine in Chapter 5 and the more elaborate version of the Aeolian harp in Chapter 3, are included for those of you who are particularly ambitious. But many of the toys, such as the vibration toys in Chapter 3 and the thaumatrope in Chapter 2 can be made very quickly and easily.

The toys in the book are safe to make, as long as you follow general safety rules and get the help of an adult when you are instructed to. Here are some safety rules to remember:

Always be sure a piece of work is securely clamped before you saw or drill. Never cut toward your hand. Never use or store inflammable materials near a burning cigarette or some other source of flame. Always work in a well-ventilated area when working with inflammable materials, and sweep up when you are finished.

## Materials Needed

Most of the tools you will need can be found in any tool-room or work shed. If you do not have some of the tools suggested, see if you can adapt a tool you have. If, for instance, you don't have a vise, improvise one from two pieces of board and a C clamp. If improvisation fails, get permission to use the tool after school in a school workshop, or borrow one from a friend. Then if you decide the tool would be useful if you had one, buy it and buy as good a tool as you can afford. Cheap tools are false economy.

The following tools make up a basic tool kit:

awl
bookbinder's folder, usually
   made of bone
bradawl
chisel (for chiseling wood)
compass
craft knives
drill (twist drill and assorted
   drills)
files
   flat file
   round file
hammer and nails
leather punch
paints
   India ink
   oil paint (black)
   transparent paint
   enamel paint of the type
      used to paint toy soldiers
paint brushes (assorted sizes)
pliers
ruler
sandpaper
saws
   coping saw
   fretsaw
   piercing saw or jeweler's
     saw
   wood saw
scissors
   one pair for cutting fabric

one pair for cutting foil
one pair for cutting paper
screwdriver and assorted
  screws

snippers
surform—a serrated-edge tool
  like a toothed file
triangle

In addition, lathe, mapping pen, pin pusher, set square, and vise would be helpful, if you can obtain them.

You will be able to find many of the materials you need around the house. If you don't happen to have something, perhaps you can borrow it from a friend. You should be able to obtain many, if not all, of the following items without buying them.

adhesive tape (assorted kinds,
  such as Scotch tape and
  masking tape)
aluminum can
aluminum foil
  foil sold in rolls
  foil from expendable pie
    dishes
bottle caps
brown paper
candle
cane (thin, split cane that
  baskets are made of)
carbon paper
cardboard (of different
  weights)
cardboard boxes
cardboard cylinders (from
  inside paper towels, waxed
  paper, etc.)
corks
cotton (absorbent cotton)
crayons

denatured alcohol
doll's clothes
fabric offcuts
  flannel
  silk
glass jars and bottles
hatbox
knitting needles (plastic and
  metal)
needles (sewing needles)
pail (plastic or metal)
paper clips
pencils
plastic bottles
plastic cup or glass
styrofoam (from packaging
  for electrical appliances)
sequins
soap flakes
stationery
steel wool
straight pins
string (nylon if possible)

sugar
  granulated
  molasses
thread
thumb tacks
tinsel
tissue paper (from clothing purchases and clothes that have been dry-cleaned)
vinegar
water glasses
waxed paper
wineglasses
wire (try raiding packing cases)
yarn

You may have to buy a few inexpensive materials, such as:

alum
aquarium (secondhand, all-glass)
beach ball
beads (plastic and wooden)
bookbinding cloth
brass knobs
brass offcuts
catgut strings (for violin or banjo)
chamois leather
chinagraph pencil
chloride of cobalt
colored paper
copper sulfate
copper tube
disks (brass, copper, or zinc)
distilled water
doll's hair
dowels (square and round, wooden)
feathers
flasks
film (photographic)
fishing weights
funnels
glue
  cold water paste
  Duco cement
  epoxy resin
  fabric cement
  impact cement
  paper paste
  plastic glue
  PVA adhesive
  rubber cement
  wood glue
glass chimney
glass sheets
glass tube
glycerin
gourds
hollow figure
iron filings
jeweler's findings
kapok
lead shot
lenses (for stereoscope)
mercury
mirrors (small)

muslin
nickel
oil of tartar
onion skin paper
paper stars
parchment
piano pins
pipe (long-stemmed, clay)
plants
plastic dolls
plastic drainpipe
plastic figures
plastic offcuts
plastic rod
plastic tubes
Plexiglas
polythene plastic
potting soil
pulleys
putty
ring (large wooden or plastic)
rivets
rubber tubing
saltpeter
sand (if not available outdoors where you live)
sealing wax
seaweed

sheet rubber
sodium silicate
stereoscope pictures
tacky putty
test tubes
tissue paper (colored)
tracing paper
varnish (polyurethane)
violinist's rosin
whistles
wick (candle)
wire (thin and thick)
  brass
  copper
  fuse wire
  iron
  stainless steel
wood
  balsa
  bamboo
  elder pith
  hardboard
  hardwood
  plywood
  softwood
wooden pole
zinc

# 2. Optical Toys

We see an object because it is giving off light, as the sun or a light bulb does, or because it is reflecting light. And sometimes what we see is an optical illusion, as with Pepper's ghost, one of the toys in this chapter. Optical toys operate as they do because of the way in which light travels and the way it reacts when it strikes different objects.

Light travels through transparent substances, such as air, in waves, and normally those waves travel in a straight line. When light strikes an object it cannot pass through, one or a combination of three things may happen. The light may be reflected by the object; it may be refracted by the object; or it may be absorbed by the object.

When light is reflected, it bounces off an object and continues traveling, either back in the direction it came from or off at a different angle, but still in a straight line. It is this reflection that illuminates an object and thus makes it visible.

If you are looking at an object, the light rays reflected from the object toward you make the object itself visible. But not all the light rays will be traveling directly toward you. Figure 1 shows the way in which reflection can work if an object, in this case a house, is near water. As shown by the lines in the figure, some of the light rays from the roof of the house travel in a straight line toward the pond. When these rays strike the surface of the water, however, they are reflected off the water and then continue traveling, still in a straight line, but at

14

such an angle that they enter the eyes of the boy, who is looking down into the water. And as a result of these light rays, he
sees a reflection of the house in the water.

When you make the camera obscura, you will see what happens when the reflected light illuminating an object travels
through an aperture the size of a pinhole. And you will see
another interesting effect when light is first reflected from and
then transmitted through a diorama picture—a picture painted
on both sides of a transparent fabric.

Light is not always reflected in the same way or to the same
degree. When it strikes a rough surface, it is reflected ir-
regularly, but when it strikes a smooth, highly polished surface, such as that of a mirror, it is reflected regularly. By
placing mirrors at a specific angle and thus controlling the di-

Figure 1. Light reflection in water

Figure 2. Light refraction in water

rection in which such reflected light travels, you can make a
periscope or the optical illusion known as Pepper's ghost. Or
you can use mirrors to create still another optical illusion—
the illusion of several symmetrical patterns, which you see
when you look into a kaleidoscope.

When a light wave is refracted by a transparent substance,
such as glass or water, it enters that substance at an angle so
that it is bent. That happens because of the angle at which
the wave strikes the substance and because the wave is traveling from a substance of one density into a substance of another density. Air, for instance, is less dense than water, or has
fewer molecules in a given amount of space than water does,
and when a light wave traveling through air strikes a pond at
just the right angle, it is refracted, or bent, by the water in the
pond.

Refraction also affects the way in which we see things. In Figure 2, for instance, the light ray illuminating the fish for the boy is refracted at the angle shown by the solid line. And because of this refraction, the boy sees the fish as if it were to the side of its true location, as indicated by the dotted line.

Scientists use the principle of refraction when they make lenses. By making glass that is curved at an appropriate angle, they can cause light waves to be refracted so that someone who is nearsighted, for example, will see more clearly. Lenses, of course, are also used in cameras, but they are expensive, so we will use them for only one of the toys in this chapter—the stereoscope.

Light is absorbed by dull-black objects—that is, it passes into the object instead of being reflected by it (and since the object is not transparent, the light is not refracted by it). Some optical toys, such as the periscope, are painted black on the inside so that light reflected from the toy itself will not interfere with its operation.

Some of the toys in this chapter work because of the way in which our eyes function. For instance, when we look at something, each of our eyes forms a separate image, each image from a slightly different angle, and it is because of this that we see things in three dimensions. This fact is taken advantage of in the creation of the stereoscope.

Also, when we see a series of rapidly moving pictures, the objects in the pictures will appear to be moving if they vary from picture to picture. That is the principle behind movie films, and it is also the principle behind several of the toys in this chapter, such as the phenakistoscope and the zoetrope.

## Periscope

Today we associate the periscope with submarines, for that is what the crew members use to see above the surface of the water. The periscope was not put to this use, however, until the last decade of the nineteenth century, when the United

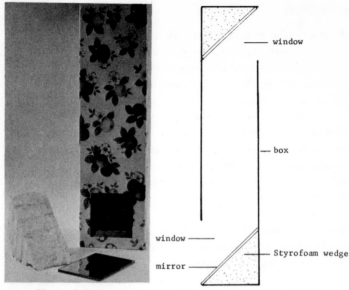

| Figure 3. Periscope | Figure 4. Parts of a periscope |

States built the first practicable submarines. But the principle behind the device had long been known to scientists.

That principle is that when light rays strike a reflecting surface at an angle other than a 90-degree angle, they are reflected at an angle. If you hold a periscope so that the receiving end faces a scene that is hidden from your view and look into the other end, you will see the scene. That is because the light rays from the scene strike a mirror opposite the receiving window and, due to the angle of that mirror, are reflected through the periscope to another mirror which you can see.

To make a periscope like the one in Figure 3, get two mirrors about $2\frac{1}{2}$ inches by $3\frac{1}{2}$ inches, such as those that come in women's handbags, and a tall cardboard box with sides about 3 or 4 inches wide, such as the kind of box a liquor bottle sometimes comes in. If the box you obtain is made of rather thin cardboard, cut some stiffening pieces, the same size as the sides of the box, out of heavier cardboard and paste them inside the box. If your box is made from good stout cardboard, however, there is no need to bother.

Cut out two square windows on opposite sides of the box, one almost at the top of the box and one almost at the bottom of the box. (See Figure 4.) Make the width of the windows the same as the width of your mirrors.

Then paint the inside of the box with India ink, laying the ink on with a brush so that the surface is dull black. When the India ink is dry, fasten the top and bottom of the box by gluing down the flaps inside the box with PVA adhesive.

Decorate the outside of the box by covering it with contact paper. To do this most effectively, fold the contact paper lengthwise around the box, so that it covers both the box and the windows and extends about 4 inches beyond each end of the box. Then snip the paper extending beyond the box, so that it forms four triangular pieces at each end, and fold these pieces over onto the top and bottom of the box. Stick the point of a pair of scissors through the middle of the windows, cut up to each corner of the windows, and turn in the contact paper, sticking it to the inside of the box. A tiny margin is sufficient. To finish the job off, cut two roundels, or rosettes, out of differently colored contact paper and stick one on the top and one on the bottom of the box.

Now to insert the mirrors. First get some thick styrofoam, the kind used to package radio parts or electrical appliances. You need a solid, rectangular block. The top and bottom must be the same size as the mirrors. If you cannot find a block that is the right size, make one by gluing layers of styrofoam together with wood glue and if necessary trimming the rough edges with a craft knife. When you have the block, take a sharp, long bladed craft knife, and cut diagonally across it from one corner to another, so that you have two pieces of styrofoam shaped like the ones in Figure 4.

Fasten these two pieces of styrofoam inside the box in the corners opposite the two windows, with the sloping sides of

Figure 5

the pieces facing the windows, as diagramed in Figure 4. Use PVA adhesive to glue the pieces in place. When the glue has set, spread some more PVA adhesive on the back of the mirrors, being careful not to smear any on the face. Glue the mirrors onto the styrofoam, and your periscope is finished.

You may even find a practical application for this toy, for it will enable you to see over the heads of people in front of you when you are having trouble seeing at a parade.

## Camera Obscura

The name camera obscura consists of two Latin words meaning "dark chamber," and the camera is in fact a dark box. In the front of the box is a small pinhole through which light passes, and that gives the camera its other name—the pinhole camera.

As the light enters through the pinhole, an image of whatever the pinhole is pointed toward appears on the inside back of the camera. However, because of the way in which light travels, the image is inverted, or upside down. This can best be understood if you look at Figure 5, in which the camera is directed toward a soldier. As already mentioned, light travels in waves, and those waves travel in straight lines. Although light is being reflected from the soldier in all different directions, only one of the rays reflected from each part of the soldier can enter the pinhole because the hole is so small, and the ray that enters will be the one that is traveling in a

Figure 6

straight line headed toward the pinhole. As you can see from Figure 6, the light ray coming from the soldier's feet is headed at such an angle that it will strike the back of the camera at the top of the image, and the ray coming from his hat will strike the back of the camera at the bottom of the image. And the light rays coming from all the other parts of the soldier will be traveling at an angle that will cause the entire image to be inverted.

The camera obscura can be used to take a picture, or it can be used to throw an image, as is being done in Figure 6. The camera is sometimes used by artists, such as the one shown in Figure 7, to throw an image of something they are sketching onto a sheet of paper, and it has been used by some famous artists. In the eighteenth century, for instance, Antonio Canaletto apparently used one when he painted the detailed pictures of Venice for which he is famous.

Figure 7

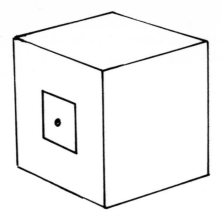

Figure 8. Camera obscura

Some camera obscuras, such as the one in Figure 6, are rather elaborate. Commercial models are available today that are equipped with prisms and lenses, and some are powerful enough to throw a picture that will cover the top of a table. Prisms and lenses do improve the camera, but they are expensive. The following instructions are for making a camera obscura that is simple and inexpensive and does not require prisms and lenses.

To make a very simple version of the toy, get a box that is about 6 inches square. If the box is not already cube-shaped, like the one in Figure 8, cut it down so it is. Paint the inside with India ink, and cut away one end wall of the box, replacing it with a sheet of tracing paper stuck down, or taped down, around the other four sides. That surface will be the back of the camera.

Cut a hole, 1 inch in diameter, in the center of the front of the camera. Cut a 2-inch square of thick aluminum foil, such as that which makes up expendable pie dishes. Make an X at the exact center of this square with a chinagraph pencil, the greasy pencil used to write on recording tapes. With a needle make a minute pinhole right in the center of the square. Paste the aluminum foil square over the aperture of the camera, or the hole in the front of the box, making sure that the pinhole is exactly in the center.

To enhance the camera's appearance, cover the outside with decorative paper, running the paper close to the hole, but being careful not to obscure it.

The camera is now finished. To operate it, hold it with the pinhole toward a brightly illuminated object. Cover your head and shoulders with a dark cloth to increase the brightness of the image and look at the tracing paper forming the back wall; you will see an inverted image of the object toward which the pinhole is pointed.

With a little extra trouble, you can make a camera that focuses. Get two cardboard cylinders, about a foot long, one just a little larger than the other. They have to fit inside one another like the sections of a telescope. The end of the smaller cardboard cylinder is closed with a cardboard circle, stuck in with PVA adhesive. A 2-inch square is cut from this cardboard circle, and on top of the space thus left is stuck a piece of metal foil, $2\frac{1}{2}$ inches square. The exact center of the foil has been pierced by a pinhole (the foil is pierced rather than the cardboard because it is easier to make a clean hole in foil).

The end of the other cylinder is covered with tracing paper.

To focus the camera obscura, point the tracing paper end at an object you want to view. Push one cylinder in and out of the other till you have a sharp picture.

If you want to make a heavy-duty pinhole camera that can take pictures, make the sides from hardboard. Using a piercing saw to cut out the pieces, make three of the sides 3 inches by 3 inches. These will form the bottom and the two sides of the camera. Cut out two more pieces, also 3 inches square, for the top and front.

You will use a piece of Plexiglas for the back. First, however, you have to make grooves in the two side pieces and in the bottom. You will slide the Plexiglas into these grooves,

Figure 9. Pepper's ghost

so make them deep enough and wide enough for you to insert the Plexiglas. Use a cabinet saw to make them, and place each groove ¼ inch from the end. Take a piece of Plexiglas and "frost" it by rubbing it with steel wool until it is semiopaque.

Using a piercing saw, cut a 1-inch-square hole in the side that will be the front of the camera. Make a pinhole in a 1½-inch square of aluminum foil and fasten it over the aperture of the camera, as you did before.

Now glue the sides of the camera together, using wood glue, and when the glue is dry, slide the Plexiglas into the back.

You can use the camera as it stands for sketching. Throw a black cloth over your head and the camera obscura to get a clear image.

Or you can take a picture with it. To do this, take a piece of black paper 2⅞ inches by 2⅞ inches, and attach a photographic plate or film to it by taping the film at the sides of the paper. Slide open the back and insert the paper with the film attached to it, the film touching the Plexiglas. Then close up the back and hold your finger over the pinhole until you have directed it at a scene you want to photograph. Choose a still subject because you will be taking a time exposure. To take the picture, remove your finger and leave the film exposed for about 2 hours if it is a sunny day or 6 hours if it is cloudy.

## Pepper's Ghost

Pepper's ghost is a theatrical illusion invented by John Henry Pepper, a professor of chemistry at the Royal Polytechnic in London during Queen Victoria's reign. As you can see from Figure 9, which shows how the illusion works, an actor covered with a sheet stands beneath the stage, where the audience cannot see him. All his surroundings are painted or draped in dull black, and if he is meant to appear headless, his head is muffled in black draperies. An assistant who is between the "ghost" and the audience but also beneath the

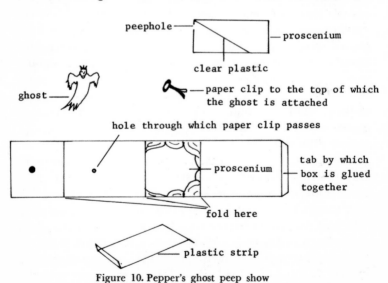

Figure 10. Pepper's ghost peep show

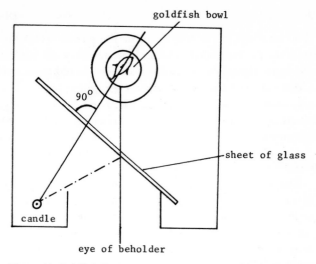

goldfish bowl

90°

sheet of glass

candle

eye of beholder

Figure 11. Goldfish in bowl (Pepper's ghost illusion).

stage has a dark lantern lighted with a limelight, a type of gas lamp. It is this type of lamp that has given us the phrase "in the limelight."

When the assistant shines the light on the "ghost," the ghost's image is reflected in a mirror next to the assistant. Because of the angle of the mirror, the reflection from the mirror travels at an angle through a hole in the stage floor and strikes a plate of glass slanted across the stage. To the audience, the ghost appears to be upstage. During Victorian performances an actor might appear onstage and converse with the disembodied ghost.

You can make a peep show, a popular toy a hundred years ago, that uses Pepper's ghost. Draw the parts for the peep show, shown in Figure 10, on cardboard and cut them out with a craft knife. Make the sides of the box 2 inches by 3 inches, and make the ghost about 1 inch tall. Paint the ghost white, the background scenery in some subdued color such as old gold, and the rest of the box making up the theater in black.

When the paint is dry, assemble the parts. To do this, score the lines of the corners of the box lightly with a craft knife, and bend them away from the score line. Fold them over with a folder so that they are a sharp right angle.

Take a slide of clear stiff plastic, the kind used to package haberdashery such as shirts, 3½ inches by 2 inches, and fold the quarter-inch tabs onto the ends of the plastic so that it can fit diagonally into the box and adhere to the top and bottom.

Now hold the box near a window, where the light will fall on one of the open sides, and when you look through the peephole, the ghost will appear to be onstage.

If you like, you can make a ghost that will move about. Make a ghost separately out of cardboard and attach it to a paper clip. Then with a bradawl, make a hole in the bottom of the box and push the clip through the hole. Bend the ends of the clip out on either side, and stick a 1-inch circle of stiff cardboard to them with PVA. By twisting the cardboard, you can make the ghost sway realistically.

You could vary the Pepper's ghost illusion by setting up a candle so that it appears to be burning inside a bowl with a goldfish swimming in it. Figure 11 shows how to set up the illusion. Make the screens, or walls, for the illusion out of sheets of styrofoam, using a craft knife to cut the styrofoam if you can't find pieces the right size. Paint the styrofoam parts with black oil paint, and when the paint is dry, glue them together.

Take a goldfish bowl and place it, with the goldfish swimming in it, at the back of the styrofoam box, directly opposite the opening for the viewer to look through. Place the candle inside the box to the left of the viewer.

Mark a straight line from the candle to the center of the goldfish bowl. Then take a sheet of glass, and place it so that it crosses the line at right angles to it. To make the sheet of glass stand, wedge it with blobs of tacky adhesive putty.

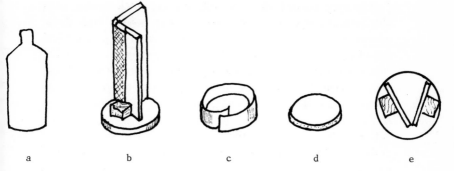

Figure 12. Kaleidoscope: (a) plastic bottle; (b) mirrors hinged with fabric and mounted on a clear plastic disk; (c) cardboard ring; (d) frosted plastic disk; (e) arrangement of mirrors from above.

Now light the candle and when you look through the opening in the front of the box, the candle will appear to be in the bowl with the goldfish.

## Kaleidoscope

The kaleidoscope has always been a very popular toy. Sir David Brewster invented the kaleidoscope in 1816, and 200,000 were sold within three months after it was patented. Since then kaleidoscopes have never quite disappeared from the playroom.

To make a kaleidoscope, select a cylindrical plastic bottle, like the one drawn in Figure 12a. Cut off the bottom, including $\frac{1}{4}$ inch of the sides of the bottle.

Now get two pieces of mirror glass cut by a glass cutter. They should be $1\frac{3}{4}$ inches by 6 inches. This size is calculated for a bottle $2\frac{1}{2}$ inches in diameter and about 7 inches high. Hinge the two pieces of glass together on their long sides by pasting them, with PVA adhesive, to a strip of tough fabric, such as bookbinding cloth.

Now get a piece of clear Plexiglas $\frac{1}{8}$ inch thick. Stand the bottle on top of it, and with a sharp-pointed awl, scribe around the bottom of the bottle to make a circle in the Plexiglas. Cut out the circle, or disk, with a piercing saw and a fine blade; then file down the circumference so that the disk can just be pushed into the end of the bottle. Cut another piece of Plexiglas exactly the same size, and make its surface opaque by rubbing it with steel wool.

Cut a strip of cardboard $\frac{1}{2}$ inch wide, and glue the two ends together so that the strip forms a ring the exact size of the inside of the bottle.

Now position the hinged mirrors on the clear Plexiglas disk as if they were two sides of a triangle. (See Figure 12b.) The two joined ends of the mirrors should almost touch one side of the disk, and the unjoined ends should almost touch the other side of the disk. When so arranged, the hinged mirrors should form an angle of about 70 degrees.

Attach the mirrors to the disk by fixing a small square block of wood behind each of them and gluing the wooden blocks to both the disk and the back side of the mirror, as shown in Figure 12e. When the glue has dried, push the disk, with the mirrors stuck on it, as far into the bottle as it will go. There should be a space $\frac{5}{8}$ inch deep between the disk and the bottom of the bottle. This space will become the object box.

Glue the cardboard ring inside this space so that its upper edge touches the disk. Now put cut-up tinsel, colored paper stars, bright spangles or sequins from old dresses, glittering beads, anything that will make a decorative pattern, inside the object box. All the pieces in the box should be less than $\frac{1}{2}$ inch thick, so they will shake about properly when the kaleidoscope is picked up.

Push the other disk, the one that has been made opaque by rubbing with steel wool, into the bottom of the bottle. It should rest against the bottom edge of the cardboard strip. Cement the disk in place with instant glue.

Figure 13

The mouth of the bottle will serve as an eyepiece. Hold the bottle up to the light, putting your eye to the eyepiece. The bright objects in the object box will display a brilliant, seven-sided pattern, each part of which is the symmetrical twin of the next. Just a shake or turn of the object box will change the pattern, and it will continue changing every time you give the kaleidsocope a shake.

Decorate the outside of the bottle with contact paper. (See Figure 13.) The neck is difficult to cover with contact paper, but you can paint it and stick paper scraps to it.

### Stereoscope

The stereoscope relies for its effect on the fact that our two eyes look at objects from slightly different angles. Our brain combines the two images, and as a result, we see depth and dimension. A stereoscope, such as the one shown in Figure 14, has a frame fitted with eyepieces which focus on a card showing two photographs of an object taken from slightly different angles. When the stereoscope is focused properly, the two

Figure 14

pictures merge into one, and instead of appearing as a one-dimensional picture, they seem to be modeled in three dimensions. For example, when the card shown in Figure 15 is viewed through a stereoscope, the two slightly different pic-

Figure 15

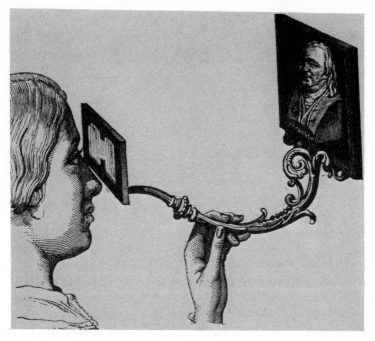

Figure 16

tures of the bust of Benjamin Franklin merge, giving the appearance of a three-dimensional statue, as in Figure 16.

The homemade stereoscope will let you join hands with the scientific toys of the past. Stereoscopes became very popular in the late 1800's, and you can buy old stereoscope cards quite cheaply in antique and junk shops. They consist of two photographs mounted on a standard-sized card that fits all the old stereoscopes. Antique stereoscopes are difficult to find, often damaged, and very expensive, but if you build your own stereoscope, you can explore the fascinating world of these old pictures.

You may have to pay an optician to make you a pair of lenses, 1 inch by 1 inch, but the cost will be a fraction of what you would pay for an antique stereoscope. The technical specifications for the lenses are as follows:

Figure 17. Shape into which mask of stereoscope is formed.

Power Approximately Flat B1/SPH+5.50
Lens Cut on Optical Center, 8 Base Out E/E 47 Pound Blank

To make the stereoscope, get some ½-inch-thick softwood, and cut out two masklike ovals with square eyepieces. Each oval is 2¾ inches high by 5½ inches wide, at the extreme measurements. The eyepieces are 1-inch square. These two ovals will be glued together with the lenses between them, like a sandwich, to form a mask, like the one diagramed in Figure 17, but first you must make a recess around the eyepieces to hold the lenses. Use a wood chisel to do this, making the recesses on the inside of each oval.

Now, using a craft knife or a wood chisel, cut away a ⅛ inch rim from the outer edge of one of the ovals. This is so it will hold a cardboard shade, which you will bend around it

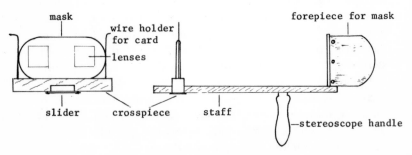

Figure 18. Parts of a stereoscope

later. Now glue the two halves of the sandwich together, so that the lenses are held between them. Do not get glue on the lenses.

Cut the staff of the stereoscope and the crosspiece out of your ½-inch-thick wood. (See Figure 18.) Make the staff 9½ inches by 1¼ inches and the crosspiece 7 inches by ½ inch. Cut a recess, 1¼ inches wide and ¼ inch deep, in the bottom of the crosspiece so it will fit over the staff.

Drill two holes ¼ inch apart, at each end of the crosspiece, placing the holes ¼ inch from the ends so that there

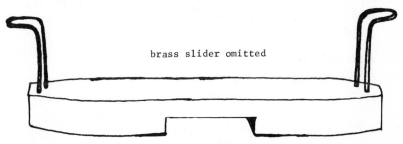

brass slider omitted

Figure 19. Frontal view of holder for stereoscope card to show how wires are bent.

are 6 inches between the two sets of holes. Take two pieces of wire, 4 inches long, and bend them to make holders, shaped like those in Figure 19, for the card. Then glue the ends of the wires into the holes, using Duco cement.

Screw the mask onto one end of the staff, making sure the forepiece, or the part of the mask with the rim cut away, faces away from the length of the staff. Take a piece of cardboard, steam it over the spout of a kettle till it can be bent by hand, and bend it around the forepiece of the mask. Secure it by forcing panel pins through the cardboard and into the wood with a pin pusher. Afterward brush it over with PVA adhesive. The adhesive will seep around the edge of the mask and form an elastic join with the wood. PVA also hardens cardboard—this will help it to stay in place.

For the stereoscope's handle use the kind of wooden handle that is attached to the tang of a file. Fit it in place 1¾ inches from the mask end of the staff and hinge it to the staff of the stereoscope, so that it can be folded flat when the toy is not in use. Cut a strip of brass, slightly longer than the width of the recess in the crosspiece. Two inches is the exact length. This will serve as a slider. Drill a hole in each end of the slider, place it over the recess, and screw it onto the crosspiece, inserting the screws through the holes in the slider. Slide the crosspiece onto the staff. You should be able to slide it up and down the staff. The stereoscope is now ready for use. Place a card in the holder and move the crosspiece until the picture is in focus.

## Thaumatrope

The thaumatrope is an eye-deceiving disk, which superimposes one image on another, relying on the phenomenon known as "continuity of vision" for its illusionary effect.

You can make one quickly from inexpensive materials, and could easily make enough in an afternoon to give away as favors at a party. Take a piece of medium-stiff cardboard that is white on both sides, and with a compass mark out a circle 2 inches in diameter. With a pencil, mark the center, or the place where the point of your compass rested, and draw a line through the center point with a ruler.

Cut out the circle with a pair of sharp scissors. Turn the circle over and draw a line exactly opposite the first one. You will use this second line later, when you draw the pictures.

Now using a bradawl, prick two holes on the line, one near each edge of the card. The holes should be about ⅛ inch away from the edge. Get two pieces of strong thread and push them through the holes, knotting them tightly, so that you have a thread tied to each side of the card. Cut off the ends, if necessary, so that the threads are about 5 inches long. The toy is held by a thread in each hand. The disk is turned around by blowing it.

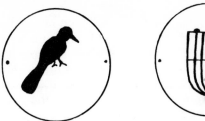

Figure 20. Thaumatrope

Now you have to draw a picture on each side of the card. The two pictures should be complementary, so that when the card is twirled around rapidly, they will coalesce and appear to blend into one picture. For instance, you could draw a bird on one side and a cage on the other, as in Figure 20. Or you could draw a jockey on one side and a horse on the other, a rose bush and a flower pot, or a rat and a trap. The rather grim subject chosen by the inventor, William Ayrton, was a hanging man on one side and the gallows from which he was hanging on the other.

Draw your picture on one side of the disk in pencil, then fill in the lines with a mapping pen dipped in India ink or a

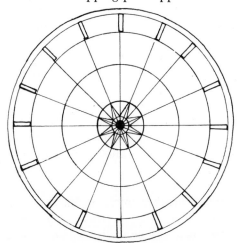

Figure 21. Disk for phenakistoscope

draftsman's pen if you can borrow one. Then draw the picture on the other side.

Draw the two pictures upside down in relation to one another, and use the center line as a guide so that the two pictures will fit together properly. For example, if you draw a bird and a cage, draw the bar that is inside the cage on one line; then when you turn over the disk and draw the bird, draw his feet on the other line. Otherwise the bird may appear to be standing in the air instead of inside the cage.

Now hold the strings of the thaumatrope tightly between your forefinger and thumb, so that the toy is at eye level, and blow. As the toy revolves, the bird will appear to be inside the cage, perched on the bar.

## Phenakistoscope

For the very little trouble required to make it, a phenakistoscope, like the one shown in Figure 21, will provide lots of entertainment. Like the thaumatrope, it works because of the phenomenon of continuity of vision. The human eye turns a series of rapidly moving images, or figures, into an illusion of continuous movement.

To make a phenakistoscope, take a compass and draw a circle with a radius of $5\frac{1}{4}$ inches on a piece of $\frac{1}{8}$-inch-thick hardboard. This will be the rim of a disk. Using the same center point, draw two more circles within the first, one with a radius of 5 inches, the other with a radius of $4\frac{3}{4}$ inches. These circles are to mark out the dimensions of the peepholes.

Mark out peepholes on the disk. There should be about twelve, with the top of the peepholes actually touching the rim. They should be about $\frac{1}{2}$ inch wide at the top, and taper slightly at the bottom.

Drill holes through the spaces to be cut out for the peepholes with a fine drill; then insert the blade of a piercing saw and cut them out. Clean up the edges of the saw cut with a needle file. Next drill a hole in the center of the disk, about

⅛ inch wide. Then cut out the disk, sawing around the rim, and finish off the edge with fine sandpaper.

Now you have to make a spindle to hold the disk. Obtain a foot length of stainless steel rod ⅛ inch in diameter. Clamp the rod in a vice, so that an inch of the top protrudes; then knock down the end with a hammer so it lies parallel with the top of the vice. It should now be at a right angle to the main part of the rod. Stain a small file handle and varnish it with polyurethane varnish. Glue the end of the main part of the rod into the handle with impact cement. Eventually, you will insert the bent end of the rod through the hole in the center of the disk and through a hole in the center of a plate, made of paper, with a series of images drawn on it.

First, however, you have to make the paper plate. Using a compass, draw a circle with a radius of 5¼ inches on heavy drawing paper. This circle will be the rim of the plate. Draw a second, concentric, circle inside the first with a radius of 4¾ inches. Cut out the plate and with a punch make a hole in the center.

You can, if you wish, make several plates and use different ones on the phenakistoscope, but you should probably begin with a simple one. For example, you could make a plate showing a juggler throwing balls into the air.

To do this, draw a juggler with his hands extended, or find a picture of a juggler in a book. The picture must be a black-and-white drawing, however, not a photograph. Get your drawing or the figure in the book Xeroxed, having eight or ten copies made. If you can't find a Xerox machine you can use, trace the figure on some tracing paper. Trace it in pencil first, then fill in the lines in India ink.

Cut out the figures, and using glue or rubber cement, paste them around the circle marked on the plate, with the juggler's feet actually touching the circle as if he were standing on the line.

Now you have to place a ball above each figure. You can

either draw the balls with a crayon or cut them out of colored paper and glue them to the plate. Place the first ball just above one of the juggler's hands, as if he had just thrown it, then place the next ball a little higher, the next one still higher, and so on until you place one directly over the juggler's head. Then begin placing them closer and closer to the other hand, as if he were about to catch the ball.

When you finish the plate, you can put the phenakistoscope together and see how it works. Put the plate aside a minute, and take your spindle and a wooden bead with a hole big enough for it to slide onto the steel rod. (You can probably get the bead from someone's discarded necklace.)

Put some glue inside the bead and slide it onto the short part of the rod, gluing it into position just before the bend in the rod. The bead will back up against the hardboard disk. When the glue is hard, slide the disk onto the rod; then slide the paper plate on also, making sure that the images face away from the hardboard disk. Fasten the plate to the disk with a few small blobs of plastic cement.

You now need a plastic bead with a hole that is just large enough for the bead to slide onto the rod and stay tightly in place. Slide the bead onto the rod so that it keeps the disk and paper plate from sliding off the rod, but don't push it so close to the disk that it prevents the disk from spinning.

The phenakistoscope is now ready for you to use. Stand in front of a mirror. Hold up the toy with the images facing the mirror and look through the peepholes at the mirror. Spin the disk with your forefinger and watch the images in the mirror. The balls will appear to move as if the man were juggling them.

Now that you see how the toy works, perhaps if you are good at drawing, you would like to make a plate on which both the figure and the ball move. Cut out a circle and make a hole as you did for the first plate. For this plate, you will have to draw two concentric circles inside the plate's rim, one with a radius of $5\frac{1}{4}$ inches, the other with a radius of $4\frac{3}{4}$ inches.

After you have made these circles, draw a man as if he were running around the plate on the circle closest to the rim. First draw him in a standing position, then with one foot slightly forward, then with the foot a little farther forward, and so on until the foot is all the way forward, as if the man were running full speed. Then show him bringing the rear foot forward a little in each drawing until, when you have drawn all the way around the rim, he is again in a standing position.

In addition to the running man, you can show a ball bouncing. Using the inner circle as a guide, place the balls in a sequence so that they appear to dance up and down.

Maybe you would like to make another plate showing a girl swinging. Get a picture of a girl on a swing, reproduce it as you did the juggler, and cut out the figure of the girl. Then draw the swing itself in the sequence of positions it would be in if someone were swinging on it. When you have finished drawing the swings, paste the figures of the girl onto the seat of the swing.

There are any number of images you can create if you want to. Use your ingenuity to think of others.

## Zoetrope

The lessons learned from the phenakistoscope can be turned to good effect when building the zoetrope, another continuity-of-vision toy.

To make a zoetrope, such as the one shown in Figure 22, get hold of an old hatbox. Using a strip of paper, 1¼ inches wide, as a pattern, draw two circles in pencil around the outside of the hatbox. The top circle should be about ½ inch below the top of the hatbox.

Draw a series of eyeholes at equal distance between the two circles. These eyeholes should be slits running at right angles to the top of the hatbox, or the drum. You can check the angle with a set square. Cut out the eyeholes, using a sharp craft knife. A band of figures inside the hatbox will be viewed through the slits.

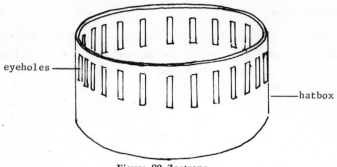

eyeholes —

—hatbox

Figure 22. Zoetrope

It is very easy to impart a spinning motion to the zoetrope. All you have to do is to find a metal tube—such as one of those aluminum tubes in which tablets are sometimes packaged—cut off 2 inches from the closed end of the tube, and fix it to the very center of the bottom of the hatbox with a good contact cement.

Now take a piece of dowel, 6 inches long and just large enough in diameter to fit into the tube. Mark an inch off the end of this tube and sharpen it to a point. The point should be cone-shaped. Glue the bottom end of the dowel into a round stand, about 1 foot in diameter and 1 inch thick, which you have drilled to receive the end of the dowel.

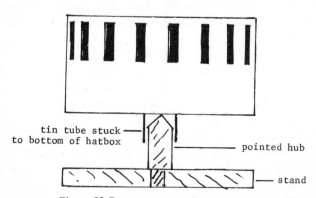

tin tube stuck —
to bottom of hatbox

pointed hub

stand

Figure 23. Zoetrope mounted on stand

When the glue has dried, you can position the hatbox on top of the dowel. Try spinning it around. The hatbox should whirl easily on top of the dowel point. Get a piece of cord about 3 feet long, tie one end around the metal tube at the bottom of the hatbox. Spin it around gently, to wind up the cord. Then pull. The hatbox will spin around and around on top of the dowel. (See Figure 23.)

I have not given precise measurements for this part of the toy because no two hatboxes are the same size. Moreover, it is good practice to adapt measurements of your own to the illustrations I have drawn. Most of my toys are made from old pieces of junk—which rarely come in standard sizes. If you have something which you feel you can adapt to making one of these toys, go ahead and try it—even if the measurements of your raw material do not square with my suggested sizes.

Now you can make the band for the inside of the zoetrope. First you have to make a master pattern. Take a piece of stiff paper and cut a strip 1¼ inches wide. Hold the strip so it forms a circle against the inside of the box, and mark the exact size of the box on the strip. Allow ½ inch overlap where the ends of the band will be stuck together, and cut off the end of the strip. Mark the position of all eyeholes on the master pattern by drawing around them with a sharp pencil.

Spread out your master pattern on a sheet of thinner drawing paper, and with a pencil make guidelines for several bands, including an outline of the eyeholes. Cut out the bands and the eyeholes. On the bands draw a succession of figures in "slow motion" just as you did for the phenakistoscope.

Paste the ends of the bands together, so that the figures are on the inside. Insert one of the bands in the zoetrope, lining up the eyeholes in the band with those in the hatbox and fastening the band with tape. When you look through a peephole, you will see the figures on the opposite side of the hatbox. Pull the string and watch them revolve. If you have made several bands, you can change them as you wish.

Making a zoetrope from an old haberdashery box is very much in the tradition of American toy making. One well-known haberdashery firm of the post–Civil War era put out a collar box that contained, in addition to a set of men's collars, three bands for a zoetrope. After a man had finished with the box, his children could turn it into a zoetrope and use the bands that came inside it.

## Praxinoscope

The zoetrope can easily be combined with a praxinoscope. With this toy, instead of viewing the moving band through slits, you observe it in mirrors covering the hub of a wheel, the wheel in this case being the hatbox. (See Figure 24.)

To change your zoetrope into a praxinoscope, you have to make a removable hub for the center of the hatbox. The hub must be as deep as the hatbox, so that the top of the hub and the box are at the same level. The hub's diameter should be smaller than that of the hatbox. You will have to find a container that is the right size and use it as a hub. An aluminum can or a plastic or metal pail would do.

The outside of at least the top half of the hub must be covered with mirrors. It is much easier to do this today than it was a hundred years ago, when this toy was popular, because

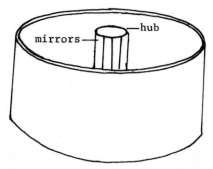

Figure 24. Zoetrope converted into praxinoscope

today you can buy small mirrors, about 5 by 2 inches—the kind that women carry in their purses or use to decorate walls.

Fasten the mirrors to the hub with PVA adhesive. Try to arrange them so that they form a continuous covering around the outside without any gaps, even if this means you have to use a smaller hub than you originally intended to use.

Now you have to make a rim to hold the hub in place. With a compass draw two concentric circles on a piece of wood. One circle should have the same diameter as the inside of the hatbox, the other the same diameter as the outside of the hub. With a piercing saw, cut out both circles, and you will have a rim.

Place the hub inside the rim to make sure they fit together properly. Then glue the rim to the inside bottom of the hatbox. The hub can now be placed inside the rim when the toy is to function as a praxinoscope and can be removed when it is to be a zoetrope. You can finish off the hub by covering the top of it with decorative paper.

Make a band or several bands without slits for eyeholds. Slip a band inside the top of the hatbox, fastening it with contact cement. When you revolve the hatbox, the figures on the band will be reflected in the mirror, and an illusion of movement will be created.

## Diorama

In 1822 Louis Jacques Daguerre and Charles Marie Bouton opened a theater in Paris, called the Diorama, where painted scenes, such as the one in Figure 25, would change from one view to another. For instance, one diorama picture painted by Daguerre showed the village of Goldau just before it was hit by a terrible landslide; this view changed to another scene showing the village after the disaster.

The two scenes were painted on the opposite sides of a fabric similar to muslin, which was hung in a theater with windows on two levels behind the stage. A ceiling separated

**Figure 25. Diorama**

the lower-level window from the higher one. A showman behind the picture manipulated these windows so that the
amount of light coming through them changed gradually,
and it was the light that determined which view the audience
would see. When the window directly behind the picture was

closed and the higher window, which admitted light to the front of the picture, was opened, that light would be *reflected from* the fabric, thus illuminating the scene painted on the front. (See Figure 25, page 46.) When the window directly behind the picture was opened and the higher window was closed, the light would be *transmitted through* the fabric, illuminating the view painted on the back of the cloth.

You can use the same principle to make your own diorama. Take a piece of muslin and paint a picture on each side of it. Use well-thinned paint which is not opaque, but which lets the muslin show through. Mount the picture on a wooden frame by fastening it to the frame with thumb tacks. You can use an old picture frame if you have one the same size as your picture, or you can make one by cutting four strips of wood with a saw and nailing them together so that they form a rectangular frame.

Hang the picture in front of a small window, such as the windows often found in the hallways of old houses. You can arrange draperies around the picture, if you want to, to make it less obvious that the picture is in front of a window.

During the day, the light from the sun will be transmitted through the cloth, so you will see the view on the back. As dusk comes on, the transmitted light will fade, and the picture will become illuminated by the reflected artificial light of the house, presenting quite a different view.

# 3. Acoustic Toys

Acoustics is the study of sound; and acoustic toys demonstrate the principles relating to the origin and transmission of sound.

## Vibration Toys

Sounds originate when an object, such as a violin string, vibrates, or moves rapidly to and fro. The vibrating object sets up waves of vibration, called sound waves, which travel through the air, or through some other medium such as water or telephone wires. It is the effect of these sound waves on our ears that causes us to hear. When the object stops vibrating, the sound waves stop also, and thus there is no longer any sound.

Sometimes, in extreme situations, the effect of the vibrations can be harmful to the ear. If, for instance, a gun were fired next to your ear, the sound waves might be enough to deafen you by harming your eardrum. But under normal circumstances sound waves are not harmful.

You can see a tuning fork—the two-pronged metal fork used by a piano tuner—vibrate. When the tuning fork is struck, the two prongs vibrate so fast that their outline becomes blurred and hazy. The sound produced is a pure tone, which the piano tuner uses as a guide when he adjusts the tones of the piano. He can stop the vibration, and thus the sound, by touching the prongs of the tuning fork.

The piano operates on the same principle. When you strike a piano key, a felt hammer controlled by the key strikes one of the piano's strings, causing it to vibrate and produce a specific tone.

Two simple toys, which will amuse young children, show that musical instruments, as well as radios and television sets, vibrate.

## String Rider

The string rider is a paper figure that "rides" on a vibrating violin string. Take a piece of paper 1 inch square and fold it. On another piece of paper draw a seated jockey, cut it out, and tape it to the folded paper so that it sits on top of the fold, as shown in Figure 26. Put the paper jockey on a violin string and draw a bow across the strings. The jockey will bounce up and down as the string on which it sits vibrates.

## Musical Figures

Musical figures will dance about in time to music on top of a piano or on the surface of a radio or television set that is emitting music.

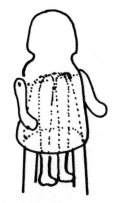

Figure 26. String rider          Figure 27. Musical figure

To make one of these figures, use a cork that is 1 inch high, or cut one so that it becomes that size. Make arms and legs by cutting them out of a piece of paper. Fasten the arms to the shoulders, or the top end of the cork, by sticking a piece of wire through the paper and into the cork. (See Figure 27.) To fasten the legs, bend two pieces of wire into a U shape, stick a wire through the top end of each leg, and then stick the wires into the bottom of the cork. The legs should be able to dangle loosely.

With an auger make four holes at right angles to each other in the bottom of the cork. Get four stiff bristles from a clothes brush or a hairbrush. Glue the bristles, which should be a little longer than the paper legs, into the holes. After the glue has set hard, trim the ends of the bristles, if necessary, so they are all the same length. The figure should stand upright on the bristles with the paper feet just clear of the ground.

Now you have to add a head. Cut the head from another cork, paint the face and hair on it in poster paint, and glue the head onto the body. You can paint clothes on the figure, or you can paint only the arms and legs and dress the figure in colored tissue paper, using some Scotch tape to fasten the tissue to the figure.

Put the doll on the surface of a musical instrument or on the radio, and it will skip about to the music—it will, of course, work on any vibrating surface, not just that of a music-producing instrument.

The Mexican Indians used to make vibration toys from wood pith and bristle that were not very different from this one. You can make any number of variations of the basic figure. For example, you could make a dancing bear or a couple waltzing together. To make the couple, you would glue their arms together instead of letting them hang loose. The man could be dressed in a smart uniform, which you could paint on, the girl in a full crinoline skirt, made from colored paper.

## Sound-Conducting and Sound-Producing Toys

As already mentioned, sound travels in waves. If you could see sound waves, they might resemble the rings you see in a cup of coffee when you drop a lump of sugar into the middle of it.

When a tuning fork or any other source of sound begins vibrating, its movement in one direction pushes the molecules of air forward so that they are crowded together. When the tuning fork moves back in the opposite direction, it leaves behind a partial vacuum, or an area with very few molecules of air in it. Meanwhile the molecules that were crowded together have pushed forward the molecules that were next to them, and they now start falling back into the partial vacuum. This crowding together of molecules, or condensation, and thinning out of molecules, or rarefaction, is passed along from molecules to molecules. In my school days, it was considered a great joke to thump someone, and then say, "Pass it on." Sound waves work the same way.

Since sound travels from molecule to molecule, it cannot travel in a vacuum. It does not have to travel through air,

Figure 28. Cardboard telephone

however. In fact, it travels faster through water than it does through the air. If young seals went to school, even those in the back row wouldn't have any difficulty hearing the teacher.

If you make a cardboard telephone, you can see for yourself how sound travels through a solid.

## Cardboard Telephone

To make this toy, as shown in Figure 28, cut two 4-inch sections from a cardboard tube, such as the tubes that come in the center of paper towels, and cover the end of each cylinder with tightly stretched parchment or rubber, lashing the parchment around the cylinder with string. These two cylinders will act as resonating drums.

Fray out the ends of a piece of string that is about 20 feet long. Attach each end of the string to one of the resonating drums by taping the frayed ends to the center of the parchment, on the outside of the drum. If you make a *permanent* join by gluing the end of the string to the parchment with PVA adhesive or rubber cement, the telephone will make a much better sound.

Give one of the cylinders to a friend to hold, and move far enough away from him so that the string stretches tightly between the two drums. While your friend holds his drum to his ear, speak into your drum, and your voice should be transmitted the full 20 feet. Once you have transmitted, you can turn the drum around and put it to your ear, and hear what your friend is saying in reply.

Although in the cardboard telephone the sound is transmitted along a solid string, that is only part of the reason it is transmitted to such a distance. The resonance imparted by the cavity of the cardboard cylinder also has an effect.

Cavities tend to increase sound, which is why some musical instruments, such as bells, have cavities, and others, such as the violin, have sound boxes. A sound box helps to amplify and prolong an instrument's sound, because the sound waves traveling inside the cavity hit the walls of the cavity, bounce back, and reinforce the sound.

In a musical instrument the walls of the cavity vibrate at the same frequency as the source of the sound—say, the violin strings. If this were not so, the sound wave would cause an echo when it bounced back instead of reinforcing the original sound.

You are probably familiar with echoes. If you make a short, sharp sound, and it bounces back from a surface that is 55 feet from you, you will hear it as an echo. To be clear, however, the echo must bounce back from a surface that is at least twice that distance from you. At sea level, sound travels through the air at 1,088 feet per second. If you are to understand an entire word, you must be some distance from the source of the echo, since no one can hear more than five syllables in a second.

Two toys illustrate the effect of cavities on sound.

## The Clucking Hen

The clucking hen can be found in Spain and other parts of Europe, but is not so common in North America. Adults here found it annoying and have called it the Devil's fiddle. I call it the clucking hen because that is what it sounds like.

To make the toy, take a plastic cup or tub and drill a small hole through the middle of the bottom. Make a knot in the end of a piece of string 18 inches long. Push the unknotted end through the hole from the inside of the cup and pull the string all the way through. Tie a knot in the other end of the string, then grab the knot that is on the inside of the cup and pull the string back through the hole again.

Holding the cup in your right hand, take a piece of violinist's rosin—the material that is rubbed on violin bows—and rub it gently up and down the string with your left hand. If the string cuts through the rosin or you have diffi-

Figure 29. Nineteenth-century speaking tube

culty holding the rosin, rub it on a piece of leather and then rub the string with that.

As you rub the string, the cup will give off noises like those made by a clucking hen. If you had just rubbed the string with rosin without having the cavity, you would never have made these noises.

### Speaking Tube

The tube is a special kind of cavity. Sound travels faster along a tube than in the open air because the sound waves are being propagated in only one direction. In the nineteenth century, a French scientist named Jean Baptiste Biot found that if a person spoke into one of the Paris water pipes, he could be heard 1,040 yards away.

You can make a speaking tube and use it like a telephone. (See Figure 29.) Since there are no batteries to run down, the toy will last for a long time, and with a speaking tube there is no chance of static on the line.

Get a piece of rubber tubing (perhaps from an old garden hose), or the outside covering of an old electric cable, about ½ inch wide and as long as you want up to about 8 yards. Buy two small straight whistles. To make the mouthpieces, get hold of a plastic bottle with a tapering neck. Detergents and liquid soaps are sold in bottles of this sort. Cut through the bottle about 2 inches down from the place where it begins to taper. Use a craft knife to do the cutting. You should now be left with a plastic funnel, wide enough to use as a mouthpiece.

Both the end of the tube and the whistle have to be fitted into the narrow end of the funnel. (See Figure 30.) Cement the end of the tube around the neck of the bottle, and push the whistle into the neck so that it protrudes inside the funnel. You may have to pack the inside of the neck with a

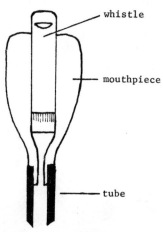

Figure 30. Speaking tube

strip of paper twisted around and stuck in with contact cement.

The whistle has to stick *tightly* inside the bottle, because you have to blow it from the other end of the tube.

When you have finished the two mouthpieces, put the whistles in place, and your toy is ready for use. You can "ring" the whistle at the other end of the speaking tube by removing your whistle and blowing hard through the mouthpiece into the tube. This will blow the whistle at the other end. A friend at that end can then remove the whistle and put his mouthpiece to his ear, and you can talk into your mouthpiece as you would into a telephone. When you have finished talking, switch the mouthpiece to your ear to hear his reply.

## Bull-Roarer

The bull-roarer is a much more elementary form of communication than the speaking tube, but it still succeeds in making itself heard. Although used in the Western world today as a toy, the bull-roarer has been used throughout history in religious rites and rain-producing ceremonies, and is still used by some primitive peoples today. The design on the bull-roarer shown in Figure 31 is a copy of the design on an Australian bull-roarer which is in the British Museum.

Take a piece of wood and draw an outline of the bull-roarer, making it an elongated oval, as shown in Figure 31,

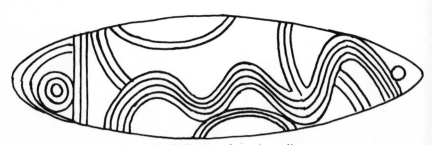

Figure 31. Bull-roarer from Australia

6 inches long and 1½ inches across at its widest point. With a coping saw, cut out the bull-roarer; then drill a hole at one end. Smooth down the wood with sandpaper, and paint a design on the toy. You can copy the Australian design if you want to, or create your own design. The bull-roarer's noise may be improved by a *carved* design, which increases wind resistance. Stick a cord about 4 feet long through the hole and tie it to the bull-roarer. Hold the end of the cord and swing the bull-roarer around and around above your head. Bull-roarers take a little time to warm up, and you may need to practice before your bull-roarer works its best; but as it whirls it will begin to make a whirring sound that will increase in volume until it is a loud roar.

The Australian aborigines made much larger bull-roarers than the above dimensions. Try various sizes until you have found the size that suits you best.

## Musical Instruments

Like all sounds, music is caused by vibration. The difference between noise and music is that noise is created by irregular, disordered vibrations, whereas musical sounds come from regular, uniform vibrations. The tone of a musical instrument is influenced by what causes the vibration, the material the instrument is made of, the thickness of its walls, and the size of the cavity. A large wide-mouthed bell of thick metal, for instance, sounds different from a small, thin-walled bell.

It is perhaps obvious that striking a percussion instrument with, say, a drumstick causes it to vibrate. The way in which other instruments vibrate is not so apparent. The tone of a wind instrument, for example, is caused by a vibrating column of air. In most wind instruments the air column starts to vibrate when the player blows into the instrument. The organ, however, is a wind instrument in which the vibration is caused mechanically.

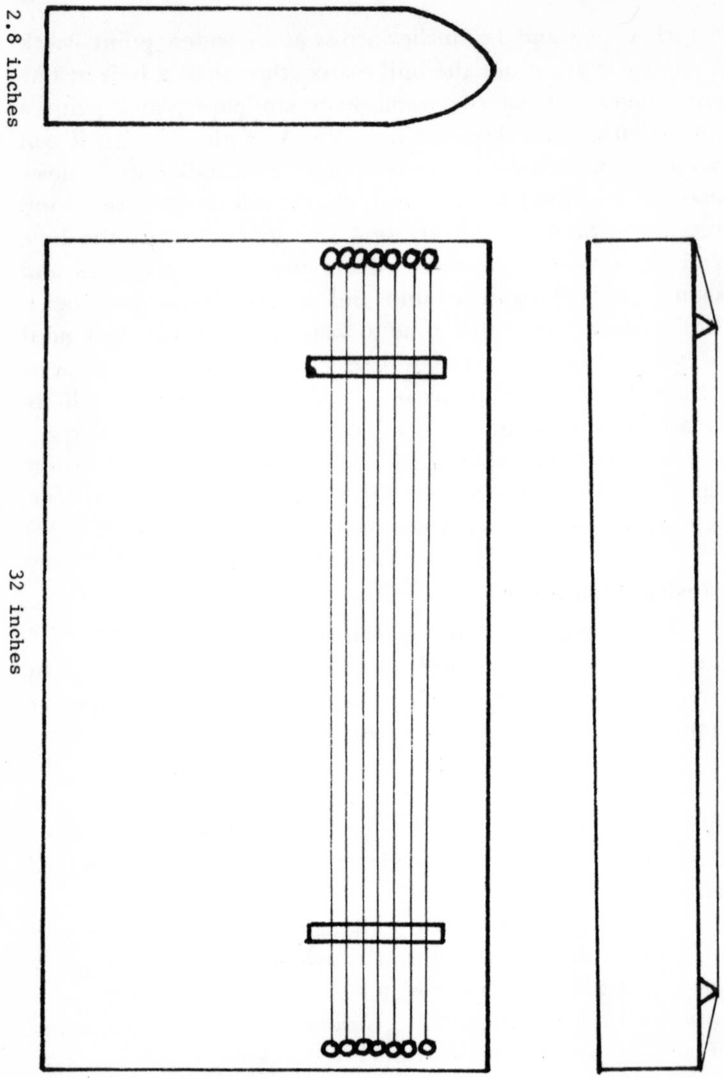

2.8 inches

32 inches

14 inches

Figure 32. Simple Aeolian harp

Figure 33. Aeolian harp from the castle of Baden-Baden

Stringed instruments produce their sounds when their strings vibrate. Thick or long strings produce low notes, and thin or short strings produce high notes. On a zither, which is a triangular-shaped instrument, you can see that the high-note strings are the very short ones in one of the corners of the triangle. Violin strings vibrate when they are rubbed with a bow. Piano strings are struck by a little hammer; the strings of the harpsichord, another keyboard instrument, are plucked by quills; and the strings of the clavichord, still another early keyboard instrument, are struck by small metal wedges called tangents. In all three of these instruments, the mechanism for vibrating the strings is controlled by the keyboard.

Harp strings are usually plucked by human fingers, but the strings of the Aeolian harp, a harp which you can make, are plucked by the wind.

## The Aeolian Harp

Not only is getting the wind to play a musical instrument an appealing idea, but in windy areas the musician is rarely unwilling to perform. Named after Aeolus, the ancient Greek god of the winds, Aeolian harps can be quite elaborate, two notable examples being the Aeolian harps that perform in the Strasbourg Cathedral and in the castle of Baden-Baden.

You can construct a simple one, however, like the one shown in Figure 32, and place it on a windowsill by an open window. First you have to construct a wooden box. Make it $2\frac{1}{2}$ inches deep and 10 inches wide, and make its length 2 inches less than the width of the window. Use thin pine for the top of the box so it will resonate, and make the sides of a $\frac{1}{4}$-inch-thick hardwood, such as oak, boxwood, or elm, so they will be sturdy.

After cutting the parts of the box to the right size, cut four circular holes in the top of the box, using a fret saw or piercing saw, spacing them so that they run at right angles to the strings in the middle of the harp. These will improve the quality of the top as a sounding board. Now you can glue the box together.

Next cut two 10-inch-by-$\frac{1}{2}$-inch bridges out of hardwood. These are for the strings to rest on. Glue them across the top at each end of the box.

Now push 8 piano pins into one end of the box $\frac{1}{2}$ inch apart and 1 inch down from the top of the box. On the other end, directly opposite the piano pins, fasten studs or rings and eyes. Attach eight strings to the pins and studs, stretching them over the bridges.

If you have had music lessons or are naturally musical, you can tune the harp yourself. If not, maybe a musical friend will help you. The harp can be tuned in harmonics, thirds, fifths, and octaves.

To operate the harp, raise the window a few inches and place the harp so that the wind blows across the strings. It takes a strong breeze to bring out the full tone of an Aeolian harp, so choose a window that is well ventilated. You can either place the harp on a table just inside the window or place it half in and half out of the window with a wedge on each side so it will not fall out.

Since making a musical instrument is an art as well as a science, those of you with musical ability may have more success with the harp than others. Perhaps you would like to construct a more elaborate harp.

The diagram in Figure 33 is of one of the Baden-Baden instruments. This instrument is 32 inches long, 14 inches wide, and 2.9 inches deep, and has seven strings. The box should be made of a thin pine or fir wood well planed so that it is $\frac{1}{8}$ inch thick, and when you glue the box together, you should be sure the joints are as close fitting as possible. Before you do the gluing, however, cut out 4 sound holes in the face of the harp, or the area that will be under the strings. Make them $\frac{1}{2}$ inch across, and space them regularly across the face of the harp.

One end of this instrument is rounded. You can do this by steaming the wood over a kettle of boiling water until it can be bent, then bend the softened wood over a rounded form such as a table leg. Lash in place with string and leave the wood to dry. It will retain its rounded shape once it has dried. The rounding of the end is supposed to improve the sound, like the bulging belly of a violin, but if you want to make it square, it will probably still sound good.

When you have finished putting the box together, make bridges $\frac{1}{2}$ inch deep and $\frac{1}{4}$ inch across out of oak, boxwood, or elm, and glue them to the face of the sounding case. Put them in place on the sounding case, then mark them with a scratch so that they are the exact length of the sounding box. Then trim them square with a piercing saw. Make the bridges pointed at the top by shaving them down with a plane. The bridges are glued to the harp, and the strings rest upon them.

Get some catgut strings and some musical-instrument pegs,

like the pegs that hold the strings in a guitar. Drill holes just wide enough to hold the pegs, in a line ½ inch in from the edge of the case. Screw them in with your fingers. Get a guitarist or violinist to show you how he fastens the strings of his instrument to the pegs and how he turns them to tighten the strings and thus tune the instrument.

## Musical Glasses

In the eighteenth century, performers in Great Britain played music on a set of drinking glasses, tuned to the scale, by rubbing the brim of the glasses with moistened fingers. Initially such musical glasses were very simple, but when Benjamin Franklin heard them played in London in the early 1760's, he was inspired to create an improved form of the instrument. His instrument was called a harmonica but was very different from the harmonicas we know today. It consisted of a series of glass bowls which fit inside each other, held together by a spindle, and were revolved through a water trough. The performer touched the moistened revolving edges of the bowls to play the instrument.

It is best to keep your homemade instrument simple, however. In fact, it takes practice to learn how to play musical glasses with moistened fingers, and you will probably find it easier to play the glasses as a xylophone. A percussion instrument, the xylophone generally consists of a series of wooden bars that are graduated in length to sound the musical scale, and is played when the musician strikes the bars with a wooden hammer. In the West the xylophone hasn't been as popular as some other instruments, but in East Asia the gamelan, which is similar to the xylophone, will often be the chief instrument in an orchestra.

To make your water-glass xylophone, get eight glasses of the same size and shape and place them on a wooden tray that has been turned upside down. The tray will improve the sound.

Figure 34. Musical notation for arrangement of glasses

Pour about half an inch of water into the first glass, slightly more into the second, and so on until you reach the last glass, which should be three-quarters full. When you strike the glasses, they will sound different tones because of the different volumes of air in the glasses. So far, however, you have only filled the glasses to approximately the correct levels. You will have to tune the glasses by adding or pouring out water until they sound the notes of the musical scale. You can ask a musical friend to help you if you want to.

After you have tuned the glasses, mark the water level on the outside of each glass, first with a chinagraph pencil, then permanently with a line of colored adhesive tape. This enables you to put the xylophone away and then set it up again without having to retune all the glasses, or if you leave the xylophone out for a while, it makes it easier for you to keep the water at the right level if it evaporates.

To play the instrument, take a small wooden hammer and strike the glasses gently on the rim. The crystalline material of the glasses makes them into natural bells.

After you have learned to play the water-glass xylophone, try playing musical glasses with your fingers. Place the glasses on a wooden tray and tune them, just as you did for the xylophone. Figure 34 gives one possible arrangement for fifteen glasses, along with a musical staff showing the notes for each glass.

You might find that wineglasses work better than water glasses, since wineglasses are usually made of finer glass. To play them, dip your finger in a little gum arabic dissolved in water, and rub your fingers around the outside of the glasses. Stand facing the glasses so that the high notes are to your right and the low notes are to your left.

As you play these glasses, you may notice that the water moves about in little globules arising from the surface and the sides of the glass. This wave motion is caused by the vibration of the glass.

## Musical Weathercock

Not only can the wind play a harp, it can also play a musical weathercock. You can make one like the one I con-

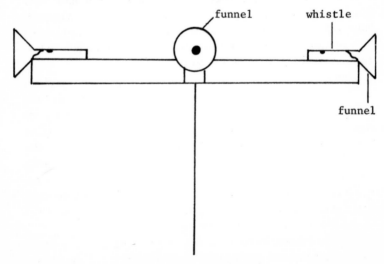

Figure 35. Musical weathercock

structed for my own garden, a diagram of which is shown in Figure 35.

You need four strips of wood, 3 feet long, 2 inches wide, and 1/2 inch thick. Join these four boards so that they form a cross. You can do this by notching two boards so that the two joints fit, then gluing them together with woodworker's strong setting glue.

When the glue is hard, drill a hole through the center of the cross, large enough for you to insert a metal rod.

Now get four straight whistles and four plastic funnels that will fit into the mouth of the whistles. Stop up all the holes but one on the whistles, leaving a different note free on each whistle. Glue a funnel into the mouth of each whistle using contact cement, and glue the whistles to the ends of the weathercock in the same way.

In addition to a metal rod, you need a long wooden pole which you will plant into the ground. Drill a hole in one end of the pole and glue the metal rod firmly into the pole.

Make a 4-inch-wide wooden disk, cutting it out of inch-thick wood, and drill a hole in the center of it. The weathercock will sit on top of this disk. Slide the disk onto the rod and glue it into place, leaving enough room for the weathercock. When the disk is firm, glue the weathercock in place above it.

The weathercock is now finished, and you can insert the pole in the ground. Be sure to position the weathercock so that the four arms face north, south, east, and west. Unlike other weathervanes, this one will not move as the wind blows. Instead, the wind will blow into the whistle, and the tone will let you know which direction the wind is coming from. Like the Aeolian harp, however, the whistle weathercock needs a good breeze to bring out the full tone.

## Chladni's Figures

Sound waves not only cause us to hear noise, they can be used to create pictures. The process for doing this was dis-

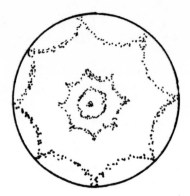

Figure 36. Chladni's figures

covered in the 1820's by Ernst Chladni—hence the name Chladni's figures.

To make Chladni's figures, take a square or round piece of opaque Plexiglas, about 1/8 inch thick and 1 foot across, and glue a 1-inch-square wooden peg in the exact center of the Plexiglas, using epoxy resin. When the glue has hardened completely, clamp the wooden peg in the jaws of a vise so that the Plexiglas plate is held immovably in a horizontal position.

Scatter a little sand or dry powdered paint onto the plate, making sure the sand or paint is a color that contrasts with the plate. Now draw a violin bow across the edge of the plate so that you produce a single tone. As you do this, the sand will begin to jump about and gradually arrange itself in a definite pattern. (See Figure 36.)

Once the pattern has emerged, preserve the design by spraying the plate with artist's fixative, shellac dissolved in denatured alcohol. Apply several coats, allowing each one to dry before you apply the next one, so that the sand is completely fixed onto the plate.

If you wish, you can frame the design and hang it as a picture.

# 4. Flying Toys

Many great inventions have started life as toys. The first automobile, for example, was a model that ran across the floor, and model planes took to the air long before the Wright brothers took off at Kitty Hawk. One early model was the orthocopter shown in Figure 37, invented in 1796 by Sir George Cayley.

Like modern-day planes, Cayley's model was mechanically driven. It was also heavier than air. Basically a modern airplane is able to fly, even though it is heavier than air, because as it moves through the air at high speed, a vacuum, or space without air molecules in it, is created above the wings, and the air below the wings pushes directly against the lower surface of the wings. Both the vacuum and the action of the air against the bottom of the wings help to lift the plane.

The airplane is an example of one kind of flying machine—the heavier-than-air flying machine. Other flying machines, such as the balloon, are lighter than air, and it is because they *are* lighter than air that they rise. These machines are filled with a gas that is lighter than the surrounding air.

The first balloons were filled with hot air. They were lighter than the surrounding air because when air (or any gas) is heated, its molecules spread apart, making it lighter than colder air. It is because there are fewer molecules in a given amount of heated air than there are in the same amount of cold air that the heated air is lighter.

The hot-air balloon was invented in 1783 by Joseph and

Étienne Montgolfier. Later that year J. A. C. Charles ascended in a hydrogen-filled balloon. Hydrogen is the lightest known gas, and traditionally it has been used in balloons. It is dangerous, however, because it can be explosive, and today helium, a noncombustible gas, is usually used in balloons. Helium is the second-lightest known gas and is about one-seventh as heavy as air. (See Figure 38.)

Both helium and hydrogen are light enough so that the weight of the entire balloon—including the car below it, the netting that holds the car, the fabric of the balloon itself, and the passengers—is less than that of the air the balloon displaces. (See Figure 39.)

Just as a cork, whose density is less than that of water, rises in water, the balloon rises in the air. When the balloonist wants to descend, he releases some of the gas from the balloon.

You can make both the heavier-than-air orthocopter and a hot-air balloon, as well as still another type of flying instrument, one that is a puzzle to scientists—the boomerang.

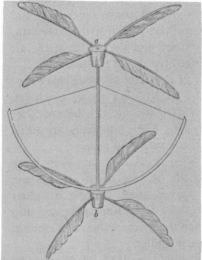

Figure 37. Orthocopter

Figure 38

## Orthocopter

To make an orthocopter, you need a plastic knitting needle about 1 foot long, two corks, a piece of slim bamboo about 2 feet long, some thin string about 2 feet long, and eight feathers about 8 inches long.

Drill a hole lengthwise through each cork. Make one hole just large enough for you to insert the rod, or knitting needle, into it. Make the other hole large enough so you can turn the rod after you have inserted it in the hole.

Now stick four feathers into the sides of each cork, placing them directly opposite each other and about ½ inch from the top of the cork. And place the feathers at an angle, like the

Figure 39

sails of a windmill. (See Figure 37, page 68.) When you have the feathers positioned properly, glue them in place. These will serve as propellers.

Next drill a hole in each end of the bamboo for the string. Drill another hole in the center of the bamboo, making it large enough so you can insert and revolve the rod in it. Glue the cork with the larger hole in it to the bottom of the bamboo, aligning the hole in the cork with that in the bamboo.

Take the other cork, and with the rod push the center of the string into the hole in the cork. Then put some glue into the hole, and glue both the string and the end of the rod into the hole. When the glue is dry, tie the ends of the string to the ends of the bamboo, inserting the string through the holes in the bamboo. Then stick the bottom end of the rod into the hole in the cork that is glued to the bamboo.

To make the orthocopter fly, turn the two corks in opposite directions. As you do this, the string will wind around the rod, and as the string becomes tight, it will pull the bamboo into a bow shape, as shown in Figure 37. When the string is tight, place the cork that is glued to the bow on a table, being careful not to let the string unwind. Holding on to the upper cork, press down with enough force to prevent the string from unwinding. Then let go suddenly, and the orthocopter will fly to the ceiling.

## Soap-Bubble Balloon

Before making a hot-air balloon powered with some sort of fuel, you can make a soap-bubble ballon. To power a soap-bubble balloon, you need only a puff or two of your own breath. Although the gas you breathe out, carbon dioxide, is not nearly so light as hydrogen or helium, it is lighter than the air in a cold room because it has been warmed by the heat of your body to 98.6 F., which is your normal blood temperature.

As long as the carbon dioxide inside the bubble is lighter than the air in the atmosphere, the bubble will rise. When it cools to the same temperature as the air, the bubble will float parallel to the ground, and finally, when the carbon dioxide becomes cooler than the air, the bubble will fall to the ground.

Before making the bubble itself, make your balloonist. Draw an inch-high figure, like the one shown in Figure 40, on very thin paper, such as onionskin, and cut it out. Also cut a round disk, ¼ inch in diameter, out of the paper. You will have to use very fine, sharp scissors to do this.

Take a fine cotton thread, 1½ inches long, and fray out the ends. With the smallest possible dabs of PVA, glue one end to the balloonist's head and the other end to the paper disk. Wipe off any surplus glue and press the thread and paper attachments between a folded layer of waxed paper, which will not adhere immovably to the glue when it has dried.

For your soap bubble, make a stiff lather of pure soap flakes, such as Ivory flakes, and water, and add a little glycerin. To blow the bubble, you need a glass tube about 9 inches long.

Take your balloonist, the glass tube, and a bowl of your soap mixture into a cold room. Dip one end of the glass tube into the soap-and-water mixture. Take a deep breath, hold it for a second or two, then blow steadily and strongly through the tube into the basin. Keep blowing, with the end of the tube pointing downward, until a perfect bubble has formed.

Then, still holding the tube pointing downward, drop the dry paper disk lightly onto the bubble, or balloon. The surface tension of the bubble will hold the disk in place, provided it is not too heavy. As soon as the disk is firmly fixed, gently turn the tube upward, and the balloon will sail away.

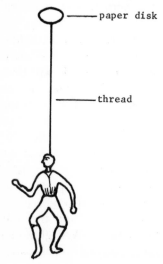

paper disk

thread

Figure 40. Soap-bubble balloon passenger

Figure 41

Indoors, the balloon should reach the ceiling. If, instead of launching it in a cold room, you launch it outdoors on a cold, frosty day, it should travel unchecked for several hundred yards.

## Fire Balloon

Now that you have seen 'that a hot-air balloon does fly, perhaps you would like to make a hot-air balloon using a controlled heat source. You should be very careful when making the fire balloon, however. Since it is made of tissue paper, it may catch fire, and it should be released only where it will do no harm if it lands in flames, such as on an empty beach with the wind blowing toward the lake or sea. *And you should never release the fire balloon unless you are with one of your parents or some other adult. The adult must always take care of the heating-up process.*

The balloon is made from twelve separate sections, so your first step is to cut out these sections. To be sure they are all the same size and shape, make one section out of cardboard and use it as a pattern. (See Figure 41.) First draw an outline on the cardboard, then cut the section out with

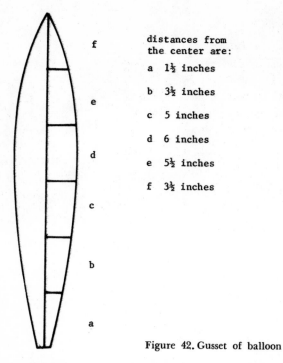

distances from
the center are:

a  1½ inches

b  3½ inches

c  5 inches

d  6 inches

e  5½ inches

f  3½ inches

Figure 42. Gusset of balloon

scissors, making it 25 inches long, about 5 or 6 inches across at its widest point, and shaped like the one shown in Figure 42. Be sure to make the bottom flat, as shown in the illustration, so that when you glue the sections together, there will be a hole at the bottom of the balloon. You will use this hole to fill the balloon with hot air.

When you have cut out the pattern, place it on several layers of tissue paper and cut around it with a craft knife. You can make the balloon decorative by using tissue paper of several different colors.

Use cold-water paste, which is sold in craft shops in powder form and is used for bookbinding, or well-diluted PVA adhesive to paste the sections together. Using a small brush so you won't get too much paste on the paper, carefully brush the paste along the edge of one section. Then put the edge of another section on top of it, fitting the two edges together so that the sections form the beginning of a sphere. Press the edges together with your fingers, then smooth down the joint with a bookbinders' folder (made of bone or plastic) or a smooth-surfaced wooden letter opener.

When you have pasted three sections together this way, you will have a quarter of the balloon. Set that quarter aside and make the other three quarters the same way. Then when the glue is dry, paste the quarters together to make two halves, and finally, join the two halves.

With your first balloon, the top of the sections may not fit together properly. To eliminate any leaks, through which the hot air could escape, cut a circular crowning piece, 3

Figure 43

inches in diameter, out of stationery. You will paste this onto the top of the balloon, but first poke a small hole in the center of it with a needle. Take a piece of thread, about 6 inches long, stick both ends of it through the hole so the thread forms a loop on the upper side of the crown, and fasten the ends to the lower inside with some Scotch tape. Now paste the crown to the top of the balloon. You can use the loop of thread to hold the balloon when you are filling it with hot air, as the boys are doing in Figure 43.

The bottom of the balloon may also look a bit ragged. You can give it a neat appearance and strengthen it by cutting a strip of writing paper, 12 inches long and 2 inches wide, and pasting the strip around the hole in the bottom. (See Figure 44.) Before pasting this strengthening strip, fasten two pieces of wire, 3 inches long, to the strip.

These wires will hold the car, or gondola, that will hang below the balloon. You can fasten them by folding the ends of

Figure 44. Balloon with car. Note strengthened strip at skirt and patch at top.

the wires over the strip, sticking a bit of Scotch tape over the ends, and then gluing the strip to the balloon. Use very thin wire, such as that used to wire flowers or fuse wire.

On your first balloon, you should probably use a purely utilitarian car, instead of making a fancy one. A metal bottle cap, such as the cap from a Coke bottle, will work well. Attach the bottle cap to the two wires hanging from the balloon with epoxy resin cement or get your father to solder the joint, and your balloon is finished.

Before trying to fly it, test it for leaks and its lifting ability. Get a friend to hold it by the loop and fill it with hot air from a hair dryer. If there are any leaks in the balloon, cover them with paper patches.

To fuel the balloon, you can use a small ball of cotton soaked in the denatured alcohol solvent used to light fondue burners or the charcoal in barbecues. Or you can steep some wick that has been rolled into a ball in melted candle wax and sprinkle it with turpentine.

Now for the ascent of the balloon. Make a small torch out of brown paper, and if you are going to use the cotton ball soaked in alcohol for fuel, put it in a jar. Take these and two fine wires, as well as the balloon, when you go out to set off the balloon.

Get your father or some other adult to hold the balloon by the loop. To fill the balloon with hot air, light the torch and hold it under the balloon, but be careful not to hold it close enough to the balloon to set it on fire. When the balloon is swelling with hot air and tugging upward, take the ball of cotton and attach it to the car, or bottle cap, by twisting the two wires around it and the car. Be sure the cotton is attached firmly so it will not come off in mid-flight. Now set the cotton on fire and let go of the balloon. It will rise majestically and soar up and away.

If you want to make another balloon, you could make a more realistic-looking car for it. Draw the car on thin paper and cut it out. Then draw one or two passengers, such as those shown in Figure 45. Put tabs on the bottom of the figures, then cut them out, and tape the tabs to the back of the car. You can add some gear, such as a drag rope or anchor, if you want to. The car holding the passengers must be slung below the cap holding the burning denatured alcohol.

A novel touch is a parachutist who will descend from the balloon. You will have to use a car that will not burn, such as the bottle-cap car. Make a parachute, shaped like the one in Figure 46, out of tissue paper, first drawing it on the paper, then cutting it out. Make a parachutist out of slightly thicker paper, such as letter paper, and attach it to the parachute.

With a needle prick a hole in the center of the parachute. Then take a thread several inches long, insert the ends of the thread through the hole, making a loop as you did for the top of the balloon, and tape the ends to the inside of the parachute. (See Figure 47.)

Now you need a slow match—that is, a piece of fuse timed to burn for several seconds. You can buy such a match or you

Figure 45. Balloon passengers. They can be attached inside the car by a dab of adhesive placed on the tab.

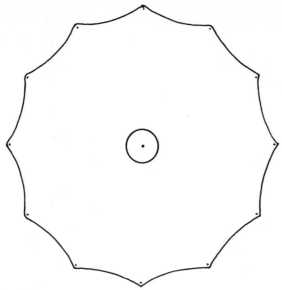

**Figure 46.** Making a parachute
Cut out a piece of paper 12 inches square to this shape. Cut out a circular patch 1 inch in diameter and paste it in the middle. Punch a hole in the exact center with a bradawl. Punch holes at each of the points of the parachute shape. Attach threads to them and tie them to the paper figure of the parachutist. Attach a thread by knotting it through the center hole. The parachute will hang from this thread.

can make one by dipping string in a saltpeter and water solution. Check your local laws before you use this—it *could* be classed as a firework.

Stick the slow match through the loop in the parachute, then tie it to the bottle-cap car, so that it forms a second loop from which the parachute is hanging. Just before you release the balloon, light the top end of the fuse, near the bottle cap. It will burn away as the balloon rises, and when the balloon is well up in the air, the lighted fuse will burn the loop in

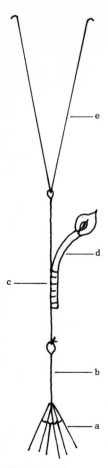

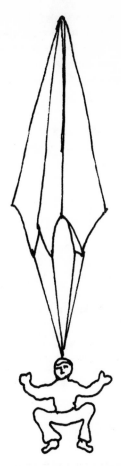

Figure 47. Descending parachutist
Attach parachute and figure (a) by
means of thread (b). Another thread
(c) has a slow match (d) tied to its
middle. It is hung by a loop at the
top to wires (e). Ignite the slow match
just before takeoff. The slow match
will burn through thread (c) and release the parachute.

Figure 48. Paper figure of parachutist
(cut out from flat card) is attached
to the car of the balloon. An ultra-
simple parachute can be made for this
figure by attaching four threads to
the corners of a paper square.

the parachute, setting free the parachute and parachutist, who will float down. (See Figure 48.)

Fire balloons can be very exciting. *Never* get so excited that you let the bottle of denatured alcohol get too near to the matches, or stand where the balloon could burn you if it caught fire.

## The Boomerang

The boomerang was often used by prehistoric peoples and is used today by the Australian aborigines, both for sport and for hunting and warfare. The aborigines are often described as the most primitive people on earth. Yet the boomerang has been a puzzle to scientists ever since it was first described in

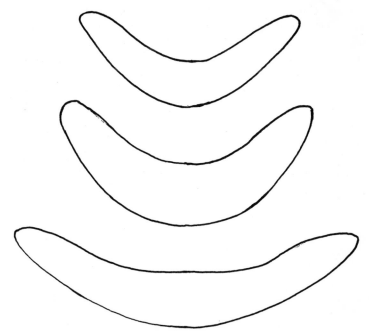

Figure 49. Boomerangs from Australia.

the early nineteenth century, and its shape may have helped to inspire the delta-winged plane.

When a skilled performer throws a boomerang, it can go as far as 180 yards, whereas 70 yards would be considered a good throw with a baseball. J. G. Wood, a researcher who became interested in scientific toys as a youngster, wrote in 1875 that when he was a schoolboy, a playmate snatched his boomerang and threw it with the wind. (Boomerangs, like aircraft, should take off into the wind.) The boomerang flew over two valleys, cut through the foliage of a lime tree, and buried itself in the lead roof of a church.

As you can see, a full-sized boomerang can be dangerous. Not only can it be a lethal weapon, it can also be suicidal, if, after you have thrown it, it comes back and hits you. It is safe for you to make a model or small boomerang, however. To study the boomerang's flying qualities, you can make a really small one, just an inch or two across, out of cardboard. Draw a boomerang shaped like one of those shown in Figure 49 and cut it out.

Now rest the boomerang against the edge of a book with the curve pointing away from you, and flick it sharply with a pencil. It will fly away, make a circle or curve, and come back to you.

After you have experimented with two or three paper boomerangs, shaped like those in Figure 49, you can make some small ones out of balsa wood.

# 5. Gravity and Balance Toys

Gravity is a force that pulls bodies toward the earth. All objects within the earth's field of gravity, from the most microscopic particle to the most gigantic boulder, are pulled by this force, but they don't all fall flat against the earth because other forces are operating on them also.

If, for instance, you hold on to a pail full of water, the pail doesn't fall to the ground, even though it is being pulled by the force of gravity, because you are holding on to it with a force that is equal to that of gravity. Of course if you held the pail upside down over your head, the water would fall, first on you, then onto the ground, because there would no longer be an opposing force to counteract the pull of gravity on the water.

When you hold on to the pail, you are counteracting the pull of gravity by pulling at the object from the opposite direction. That is only one of the ways gravity is counteracted. An object can also be pushed away from the earth's gravitational pull.

If you put the pail on a picnic table, the table is of course between the pail and the earth, with its gravitational pull, but that is only part of the story. The table pushes at the pail with a force that is equal to the force of gravity. When you hold the pail right side up, the bottom of the pail pushes at the water at the same time that gravity pulls at it, and the two forces counteract each other so the water stays where it is. And if you fastened some sort of lid onto the top of the pail, you could then hold the pail upside down over your head without getting wet because the lid would push against the water and counteract the force of gravity.

When you put objects on a table or liquids in a pail, it's so obvious they aren't going to fall to the ground that you don't even think about it. But sometimes the force that is holding an object up isn't so obvious.

Take a plastic pail outside (in case you make a mistake the first time) and put just an inch of water in it. Then hold the pail in one hand and swing it up into the air in a circle as fast as you can. The water will stay in the pail even when the pail is upside down and even though there isn't any lid on the pail to push against the water.

Why? Because a force equal to the force of gravity is pushing at the water and thus counteracting the gravitational pull. That force is called centrifugal force, and it is centrifugal force that makes the whirler, the first toy discussed in this chapter, work. When an object rotates rapidly, the centrifugal force created by that rotation acts to make the object fly off into the air instead of following its circular path. Centifugal force isn't the only force pushing or pulling the object, however, so it doesn't fly off into the air unless the centrifugal force is stronger than all the other forces, but in the whirler it does force the doll's arms and legs to stand out at an angle.

And in the pail you just swung over your head, the centrifugal force acting to make the water fly off into the air counteracted the gravity acting to make it fall to the ground. Or didn't it? If you got wet instead, you didn't rotate the pail fast enough. The faster the object rotates, the stronger the centrifugal force is, and the centrifugal force has to be at least as strong as the force of gravity to counteract it.

Scientists consider the force of gravity as acting on a definite point, called the center of gravity, within an object, and any object can be suspended in midair if it is supported directly beneath its center of gravity. This is perhaps clearest in a

Figure 50

simple beam balance. A beam, or uniform bar, is placed on a support, called a fulcrum, just as a beam is placed on a fulcrum in the lever shown in Figure 50. In the beam balance two pans that weigh exactly the same are placed on the beam, one on each end. They balance because in a uniform bar the center of gravity is at the bar's midpoint, and the fulcrum, which supports the bar at its midpoint, is directly beneath the center of gravity. The two weights are maintained in equilibrium. If, however, the two pans do not have the same weight, the beam's center of gravity will no longer be at its midpoint, and unless the fulcrum is moved to the new center of gravity, the heavier end will descend below the lighter one until the beam hits some surface.

That is the situation in Figure 50, where the force at one end of the lever is greater than that at the other end. But equilibrium can be attained with the lever also. If the person holding the other end of the lever pushes down with a force equal to the force of the weight, the fulcrum will be beneath the center of gravity, and the lever will be in a state of equilibrium.

It is because objects can be sustained in equilibrium when supported below their center of gravity that all sorts of balancing tricks can be done. The boy in Figure 51, for instance, can balance a stick on the end of his finger as long as he keeps the stick's center of gravity directly above his finger. And the French tightrope walker Charles Blondin was able to cross Niagara Falls on a tightrope, carrying a long pole weighted at both ends, because he balanced the pole so that his center of gravity was always directly above the rope.

Two toys in this chapter, the balancer and the balancing horse, work because the forces operating on them are in equilibrium. The magic stair walkers, however, tumble down the

Figure 51

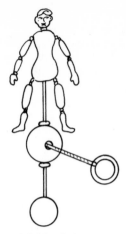

Figure 52. Whirler before costuming

stairs because the forces operating on them are *not* in equilibrium.

Gravity, then, can be a source of amusement, but it also has a practical value. When gravity is properly harnessed, it can be used as a source of power, as illustrated by the sand machine, a toy in which the force of gravity is used to power a small turbine engine.

## The Whirler

An old-fashioned toy that can no longer be bought, the whirler appeals particularly to younger children, although it is too difficult for them to make. Perhaps you would like to make one for a younger brother or sister.

First you have to make a jointed doll like the one shown in Figure 52. Use a craft knife to carve the body, limbs, and head out of soft wood blocks. Make the body about 4 inches long and 4 inches around the waist. Make the limbs about ½ inch thick, the thighs 2 inches long, the lower legs 2 inches long, the upper arms 1½ inches long, and the lower arms 1½ inches long. Make the head 2 inches in diameter.

Paint the face and hair on the head. While you are waiting for the paint to dry, drill a hole, large enough for you to insert a metal knitting needle, in the bottom of the body. Then, when the paint is dry, glue the head to the body.

Now you have to make joints for the limbs, and fasten them together and to the body. For each joint you need two pieces of wire about 1 inch long. Twist these wires so they are U-shaped. Make two holes in the ends of the limbs where they are to be joined, and in the body where the limbs are to be attached.

Take one of the limbs, say, one of the thighs, and glue the ends of one of the wires into the two holes at the top. When the glue is dry, stick a second wire through the loop formed by the first so that the two wires are hooked together. Then glue the ends of the second wire into the appropriate holes in the body. Join the other parts together in the same way. Glue a knitting needle, about a foot long, into the hole in the bottom of the body.

Dress the doll in loose-fitting doll's clothes, perhaps the clothes of a clown, cutting a hole in the seam of the trousers for the knitting needle.

Now you have to make the pull mechanism for the toy. This will be similar to the mechanism you made to revolve the zoetrope. In addition to two plastic beads and some strong thread, you will need a hollow ball. A table-tennis ball can be used to make this toy, but the more substantial the ball, the longer the life of the whirler. Any large nut such as a walnut—which can be bored and the kernel removed through the hole with a bent wire—will be ideal.

Drill a hole in the top and bottom of the ball. Make the holes so they are directly opposite each other and large enough for you to slide the ball onto the knitting needle. Drill another hole in the side of the ball.

Slide one of the beads onto the knitting needle and glue it to the needle just below the point where the figure's feet reach when they dangle. When the glue is hard, slide the ball onto the needle so that it touches the bead. Then slide the other bead onto the knitting needle and glue it below the ball.

Now you have to wind the thread around the needle; this will be a little tricky because the thread has to go inside the ball. Tie the end of the thread to a piece of fuse wire about 3 or 4 inches long. Insert the wire through the hole in the ball, pushing it far enough back so that the end can be maneuvered around the needle. (It may help if you bend the wire a little before putting it into the hole.) Maneuver the wire until it has bent back around the needle and found its way out of the hole again. Haul the wire out and untie the thread or cut it away from the wire.

Make a slip knot and pull the thread tight, so that it is fastened around the knitting needle. Then put some fabric cement on the end of the thread, and also put a dab of the cement on the knot. This will keep the knot from untying.

Tie a plastic or wooden ring, large enough for a child to put his finger through, to the end of the string. To wind the string around the knitting needle, hold the string out at a right angle to the needle and slowly turn the needle, letting the string wind onto it.

Now the toy is ready to be used. Hold the bottom of the whirler firmly in one hand and pull the string with your other hand; the figure will whirl around, throwing out its arms and legs. If you slacken the string when it is nearly all pulled out, the impetus of the figure whirling around will cause it to wind itself up again, and you can go on whirling the toy for a long time without rewinding it by hand.

## Balancer

Since the center of gravity in a heavy object is usually near its base, a heavy object that can be rocked to and fro will always return to its original position. Sometimes rocking stones are found in nature, when a large boulder rests on a natural fulcrum, such as a ridge of rock. When such a boulder is given a push, it rocks back and forth and eventually returns to its original position.

The same is true of balancers, such as the one shown in Figure 53. Balancers are great favorites with younger children. You can make two of them, using a round lead weight, the kind used by deep-sea fishermen, and two small plastic figures. Buy the largest-sized lead ball you can and any sort of figures you want, such as two dolls or plastic toy soldiers.

Using a hacksaw, cut the lead ball in half. As lead is poisonous, try to get the assistance of a fishing-tackle shop to do this for you. A safe alternative to lead for younger children is a large steel ball bearing, halved. Put this in a vise, and cut it in half with a hacksaw. It will take longer to cut through

Figure 53. Balancer

the steel than lead, but it will be quite safe for the child to handle.

The two halves will serve as the bases for the toys. Paint them first with a primer, then with a brightly colored paint. Glue one of the figures to the flat surface of the half hemisphere. When the glue is hard, the balancers are finished. No matter how hard you push them, they will always come back to rest upright.

You can make larger balancers with a beach ball and two hollow plastic dolls. Cut the beach ball in half and fill each half with sand. To make a top for these bases, take a sheet of plastic, and with a craft knife, cut out two circles with a slightly larger diameter as the top of the bases. With contact cement glue one of these plastic circles to the rim of each half of the beach ball. Then glue a plastic doll on top of each base.

A Japanese version of the balancer takes the form of a man, carved out of wood, whose arms are folded and who has no legs, just a rounded base. The figure represents the hermit Daruma, who, it is said, stood on one spot for so long that his legs withered away.

You can make a simple version of the Daruma with a dried, pear-shaped gourd. First drill a hole in the top of the gourd. Then take some pieces of lead shot, coat them with instant glue, and drop them one by one into the hole. They should stick to the bottom of the gourd. Shake the gourd from time to time as you drop in the shot, to be sure all the pieces fall to the bottom.

Give the glue time to set, then shake the gourd to make sure all the shot has stuck. If it has not, drop a little more glue through the hole.

Once again, you may decide not to use lead at all, because it is toxic. I have been handling lead weights for years, and they have always done more harm to the fish I was trying to catch than to me, but if the toy is intended for a small child— small children often like to batter their toys to bits—take

Figure 54. Traditional Japanese Daruma doll

precautions. For extra safety, use heavy gravel, the kind sold in pet shops to put in fish tanks, as the ballast for this toy, gluing it in the way I have described. Now paint the Daruma's face and arms, as shown in Figure 54, on the gourd. First use primer paint, then different colored paints.

For a more elaborate Daruma, carve the pear-shaped figure out of a soft wood, such as yellow pine. When you have finished carving it, smooth down the surface with sandpaper. Then drill a hole an inch deep in the exact center of the base, using an inch bit. Wind up some lead strip until you have a roll the size of the hole, and glue it into the hole. Now paint the figure, first in primer, then in lifelike colors.

## The Balancing Horse

Since a prancing horse poised on its hind legs is positioned on one side of its center of gravity, such a figure would normally fall over. In the balancing-horse toy, however, a counterbalancing weight is added to the other side of the figure's center of gravity, so that the horse rocks, as the balancer does.

Draw a figure of a horse, like the one shown in Figure 55, on a plank of wood 1½ inches thick. Make the figure 8 inches tall and 6 inches across. These figures are approximate, and the size of your horse will depend on the way you sketch it out on the block. You may, for example, decide to give it a long, flowing tail.

Cut out the figure, doing all the sawing with a coping saw. If you separate the legs, take particular care not to break them. You may decide to cut out the horse with front and back legs joined together.

Rub off the rough edges of the newly sawed wood with a round file. Then smooth down the wood, first with coarse, then with finer sandpaper.

Stand the horse on a table, placing it at the edge, to make sure it will stand properly on its hind legs and overhang the edge. If not, trim the bottom hooves where they touch the table, using a craft knife and a file, till the horse is standing properly.

Figure 55. Block-cut balancing horse. Figure 56. Balancing horse (fully finished model).

Drill a hole in the belly of the horse, where the cinch of the saddle fits the horse. Glue a piece of stiff wire, which may be as much as $1/8$ inch thick, into the hole, and bend the wire into a curve shaped like the curve in Figure 56.

To the end of the wire glue a lead fisherman's weight about 1 inch in diameter, and approximately the same weight as the horse figure. Check for balance by placing the figure on the edge of the table. If the figure does not balance, change the position of the wire.

Paint the whole figure, including the wire and the weight, using a primer first. When the paint is dry, put the horse back on the table. A slight touch should set the horse rocking so realistically that it will appear to be about to prance into space.

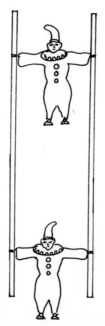

Figure 57. Magic stair walkers

## Magic Stair Walkers

To make magic stair walkers, get two plastic dolls about 2 inches high, cut off their arms, and drill a hole through their bodies at the shoulders. Push a piece of thin wire, 1 inch longer than the breadth of the shoulders, through the holes in each of the dolls.

Now get two plastic tubes about ¼ inch thick and 4 inches long and some bb's. Stop up one end of the tubes with plastic putty and pour enough bb's into the tubes so that there is about an inch of bb's in each tube. Then close the open end of the tubes with plastic putty.

Wrap small cylinders of thin cloth around the wires sticking out of the figures' shoulders to make the wires look more like arms, but do not let this cloth interfere with the movement of the figures, which should swing freely on the wire. Wind the ends of the wires around the plastic tubes, so that the figures are firmly in place. (See Figure 57.)

Now you have to make a set of stairs for the stair walkers to tumble down. You can make the stairs by just piling boxes on one another, but all the steps must be the same height. They should be about 3 inches high and about 3 inches wide. You can also make stairs from a piece of cardboard 3 feet by 1 foot. Score the cardboard at regular 3-inch intervals with a craft knife, then bend it into a series of steps. Support the steps underneath with styrofoam blocks cut from junk packaging.

To start the stair walkers moving, place both of them on the top step and then push the foremost figure, sending him down onto the second step. As he reaches it, the bb's will run to the bottom of the tube, and the shift in the weight will jerk the top of the tube up into the air, causing the second stair walker to swing over the first and descend onto the third step. Again the bb's will run to the bottom of the tube, and the first figure will swing down onto the next step, and so on until the figures reach the bottom step.

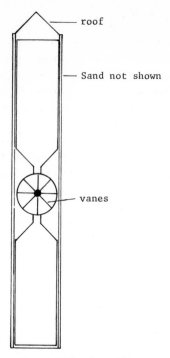

Figure 58. Sand machine

## The Sand Machine

In the sand machine, gravity is used as a source of energy to operate a turbine, which is a rotary engine. The sand machine has two sand-filled containers, just as an hourglass does, and when the sand machine is turned so that the sand is in the top container, the sand falls into the bottom container, also as in an hourglass, because of the force of gravity. In the sand machine, however, there is a spindle with vanes attached to it (like that shown in Figure 58) between the two containers, and as the sand falls it hits the vanes, causing them to revolve. The revolving spindle can be used as a source of power. If, for instance, you attach the vanes of a windmill to the spindle, this sand turbine will cause the windmill's vanes to revolve.

To make a sand machine, or sand turbine, you need a piece of plastic drainpipe about 2 feet long and 4 inches in diameter, two plastic bottles 9 inches long and $3\frac{1}{2}$ inches in diameter, a wooden dowel $\frac{3}{4}$ inch in diameter and just long enough to fit inside the drainpipe crosswise, a plastic knitting needle, three plastic beads with holes large enough for you to insert the knitting needle, some rigid plastic sheet, and a smaller piece of plastic drainpipe just over 6 inches in diameter and about the same length.

First make the spindle and the turbine vanes. To do this, drill a hole large enough to insert the knitting needle through the axis of the dowel. Insert the knitting needle into the hole to make sure it fits properly. One end of the knitting-needle spindle should stick out about $\frac{3}{4}$ inch, and the other end should stick out far enough to slip on a bead. You can remove the spindle while you attach the vanes.

Using a piercing saw, cut the vanes themselves out of the plastic sheet, making them $1\frac{1}{2}$ inches wide by 3 inches long. You will need four of them. Now you have to attach them to the dowel. To do this, take a saw and cut into the dowel where you want to insert the vanes. (See Figure 59 for the positioning of the vanes.) Make the saw cut just large enough to insert the vanes.

Later you will insert these vanes inside the small piece of drainpipe, which will form a vane housing, so check at this point to be sure that when the vanes are inserted into the saw cuts, the entire unit will fit inside the vane housing. You should be able to rotate the dowel without having the vanes touch the inside of the housing. If the vanes do touch it, make the saw cuts in the dowel a little deeper. Then glue the vanes into place.

Now you have to drill two holes in the 2-foot drainpipe, one on each side, though which the spindle, or knitting

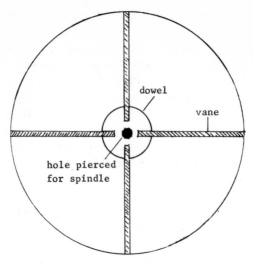

Figure 59. Spindle and vanes for sand machine

needle, will be inserted. Be sure they are directly opposite each other.

To be sure the vanes and this 2-foot drainpipe fit together properly, slide the dowel into the drainpipe, lining up the hole in the dowel with the holes in the pipe, and stick the spindle through the holes in the pipe and dowel. The turbine vanes should revolve freely inside the drainpipe.

Now you can make the vane housing. This housing will direct the flow of the falling sand so that none of the force of the sand will be wasted. As indicated above, you use the smaller piece of drainpipe for the housing. This will be inserted inside the 2-foot drainpipe, with the open ends toward the inside of the larger pipe, but as you will see when you try to insert it, you will have to cut back the ends of the smaller pipe to make it fit. Cut back a little at a time until it does fit, making the fit as snug as you can. (Remove the spindle and turbine vanes before you do this.)

Now you have to cut a hole in the top and bottom of the housing. These holes should be just large enough so you can insert the mouth of the plastic bottles. If they are too large, some of the sand will fall through the crack into the empty space between the bottle and the drainpipe, so you should make the fit as close as you can.

Also you have to be sure before you cut out the holes that they will line up properly with the mouth of the bottles when the sand machine is put together. To do this, take some carbon paper and, using some Scotch tape to fasten it, cover the mouth of the bottle with it, making sure the carbon side of the paper faces away from the bottle. Next insert the bottle in one end of the drainpipe. Insert the vane housing in the other end, pushing it in so that it touches the bottle. Then, holding the vane housing in place, twist the bottle back and forth in a semicircle, and the carbon will make an outline of the bottle's mouth on the housing. Make an outline for the second hole in the same way, but be sure the two holes are directly opposite each other.

Use a sharp craft knife to cut out the two holes.

The pieces of the sand machine are now ready to be assembled, but putting them together will be a little difficult, so perhaps you should do it once without any glue. Put the dowel and turbine vanes inside the vane housing. Then slip the housing, with the vanes inside it, into the plastic drainpipe, line up the hole in the dowel with the holes in the pipe, and insert the knitting needle. Push the knitting needle, or spindle, through so that one end sticks out just far enough for you to glue a plastic bead to it. The other end should stick out ¾ inch.

Check at this point to be sure the turbine vanes will revolve freely inside the housing. (You may have to hold the housing to do this, since it hasn't been glued in place yet.)

Now take one of the plastic bottles and stick it in one end of the drainpipe, inserting the mouth of the bottle just slightly into the hole in the vane covering. Be careful not to push the mouth of the bottle in too far. If you do, it will touch the turbine vanes and prevent them from moving. It may be easier to get the bottle and vane covering to fit just right if you reach into the other end of the drainpipe and hold the vane housing in place as you manipulate the bottle.

Check to be sure the vanes still rotate freely. Then put the second bottle in the other end, again inserting the mouth just slightly into the opening in the vane housing and checking to be sure the vanes rotate properly.

Once you have the knack of putting the unit together, you can glue the pieces in place as you assemble them. Put the turbine vanes inside the housing, as you did the first time, but before you slip the housing inside the drainpipe, put a dab of PVA glue inside the dowel. Then, working quickly so the glue doesn't dry before you have finished, slip the vanes and the housing into place and insert the spindle, making sure the ends stick out the proper distance.

When the spindle and dowel are glued firmly together, put a ring of glue around the seams between the vane housing and the inside of the 2-foot drainpipe. Make sure the housing is positioned so that the spindle revolves freely, then put the 2-foot drainpipe on its side, so the vane housing will not move, and let the glue dry.

Meanwhile fill one of the bottles with sand. Use only dry, clean sand. (To be sure the sand is completely dry, you could place it in a baking pan and put it in an oven set at 200 degrees for an hour or two.) If you live in a state like Arizona, you have an advantage, for sand from a dry area, such as a desert or sand dune, is better than water-borne sand. That is because sand from such areas is abraded as it is blown about and therefore doesn't have sharp edges that can cut. Water-borne sand, on the other hand, has sharp angular edges because the water cushions the grains of sand as they are carried against each other and against rocks. Such sand can be a sharp cutting medium that will wear out your sand machine.

Sift any sand you collect yourself, to make sure that it contains no vegetable matter or insects, before you put it in the bottle.

After filling the bottle with sand, put some glue around the outside rim of its mouth, to glue it to the vane housing, and some glue on the outside of the main part of the bottle, to glue it to the drainpipe, and insert it in the bottom end of the drainpipe, making sure the mouth of the bottle and the vane housing are fitted together properly.

Wait for the glue to dry, then glue the empty bottle into the other end.

When both bottles are glued firmly in place, glue one of the beads to the short end of the spindle, making sure that the spindle is still able to revolve. Glue another bead to the 3/4-inch end of the spindle, sliding the bead on so that it is next to the drainpipe but does not prevent the spindle from revolving.

When all the glue is hard, turn the sand machine so the empty bottle is on the bottom, and the sand will fall onto the

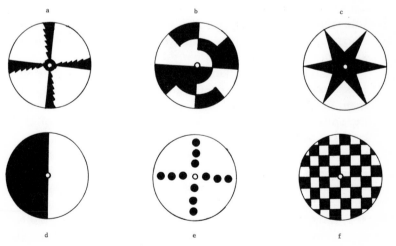

Figure 60. Magic circles

turbine vanes. If the vanes do not start to move right away, start them revolving by moving the spindle manually. The sand will continue to fall, first onto the vanes, causing them to revolve, and then into the bottom container.

Now that you have this miniature engine, how do you want to use it?

You can, if you wish, decorate it to look like a windmill and attach the vanes of a windmill to the spindle. These will revolve as the spindle turns. To decorate it, you can make an ornamental top, shaped like a roof, out of cardboard. Make the roof detachable so you can move it from one end to the other when you turn the sand machine over. Paint tiles or slates on the roof, and paint the rest of the sand machine, perhaps painting windows on two sides.

Make the windmill vanes from plastic sheeting. Cut two fine slots in a cross shape with a fretsaw on the end of the spindle, and slot in the vanes at right angles to one another.

If you would rather not make a windmill, you can attach magic circles, such as those shown in Figure 60, to the spindle. These magic circles are still another form of optical toy. When they revolve, the pattern drawn on them appears to change, just as the figures in the zoetrope or on the phena-kistoscope appear to move when they revolve.

Make the magic circles out of thin cardboard. Using a compass, draw the circles with a diameter of 4 to 5 inches, cut them out, and punch a hole, large enough for you to insert the spindle of the sand machine, in the exact center of the circles. Then draw a design on each circle.

Slip one of the completed circles onto the ¾-inch end of the spindle. Hold the circle in place by slipping a plastic bead onto the spindle. Then start the sand machine operating and watch the magic circle revolve.

You can make the designs in black and white, using India ink, or in color, using poster paint. Or if you prefer, you can use colored paper with adhesive backing. There are numerous designs you can use for your circles, some of which are shown in Figure 60.

For instance, you can paint a six-pointed red star on a white background (Figure 60c). When the circle revolves, the two colors will merge so that the red will appear at the center and gradually change, from the center outward, to lighter shades of red and pink, and the outer edge of the circle will appear white.

Or you can paint one half of the circle red and the other half green (Figure 60d). When this circle turns, the two colors will merge to form brown. If you draw seven segments radiating from the center of the circle and paint them red, orange, yellow, green, blue, indigo, and violet, they will combine to form gray when the circle revolves.

Another possiblity is to draw a cross, making one edge of each arm jagged like a saw blade (Figure 60a). When this design revolves, a series of circles will appear, those nearest the center of the magic circle being the darkest, those nearest the circumference the lightest.

If you want to make the design shown in Figure 60e, draw a cross, its arms intersecting at the center of the circle, in pencil. Then, using these penciled arms as guides, paint the black dots at measured intervals. When this circle turns, the dots will appear to join together and form concentric circles.

Perhaps you can guess how the designs shown in Figures 60b and 60f will change. You can copy these also and use them on your sand machine.

Although the origin of magic circles is obscure, we know they were given a practical application in the early twentieth century, when phonograph buffs used such circles to check the speed of their machines. Later magic circles that were driven by electric motors were used in advertising displays in store windows.

# 6. Heat Toys

When heat is transferred from one substance to another, it raises the temperature of the second substance and causes changes in its physical characteristics. If the substance being heated is a gas, its molecules move apart so they are less dense, and therefore the gas becomes lighter.

As you saw when you made the hot-air balloon discussed in Chapter 4, heated air rises, since it is lighter than the surrounding air. Thus when you turn on a radiator, the air immediately above it rises because that air is heated before the neighboring air and therefore is lighter than the surrounding air. As the heated air rises, the cooler, heavier air moves in to replace it, forcing it up farther. As this cooler air moves in place immediately above the radiator, it too is heated and begins to rise as it becomes lighter. The resulting current of moving air is called a convection current, and it is convection currents that make two toys in this chapter operate—the spinning snake and the windmill figure.

You are probably familiar with heat conduction. If, for instance, you pick up a hot potato from a barbecue pit, the heat is transferred directly from the potato to your hand through conduction. It is also through conduction that the air immediately above the hot radiator is heated—that is, the heat is transferred directly from the radiator (or possibly from the hot radiator cover) to the air.

Another way in which objects can be heated is through the absorption of radiant energy, which is energy carried in waves, such as light waves. Dull-black objects absorb light waves readily and thus also absorb radiant energy. You may have noticed that if you pet a black dog on a hot sunny day his coat feels hotter than other surfaces nearby. That is because his coat absorbs the radiant energy coming from the sun. Other surfaces, such as a silvered, highly polished one, reflect light rather than absorbing it and therefore do not absorb radiant energy in the same way that black surfaces do. This difference in the capacity of surfaces to absorb radiant energy is used to build an instrument that measures the intensity of radiant energy—the radiometer. Perhaps if your science teacher will help you, you will be able to make your own radiometer.

## The Spinning Snake

To make a spinning snake—a snake that twirls constantly when hung above a hot radiator—take an aluminum pie plate (the kind store-bought pies come in) and cut off the sides of the plate with a pair of scissors that you save for cutting aluminum foil. Using a chinagraph pencil, outline the snake (See Figure 61), on the bottom of the pie plate. Starting at the tail, cut out the snake's body by cutting along the line you have drawn. Then with a bradawl make a small hole, large enough for you to stick a needle and thread through it, right in the center of the snake's tail.

Before inserting the thread, paint the snake with a quick-drying enamel, either in natural colors or in stripes. Stripes will be particularly effective when the snake begins to spin.

Figure 61. Spinning snake

Or if you want to make an elaborate snake, cover it with sequins, gluing them on and placing them in layers of alternating green and gold, with the layers overlapping so the sequins look like scales, and give it eyes by gluing on two beads.

While the thread is still on a spool, unwind it slightly and stick the end through the eye of a needle, then stick the needle through the hole in the snake. Pull the thread through, remove the needle, and tie a knot in the end of the thread so it won't slip back out. Unwind the thread from the spool until it is long enough for you to hang the snake from the ceiling. The snake should dangle just above the radiator. Then cut the thread and tie a knot in that end.

Hang the snake over your hottest radiator, fastening the end of the thread to the ceiling with a tacky substance such as putty rubber, or with scotch tape. After you have hung the snake, give it a shake to be sure all the coils are hanging freely.

As the convection currents strike the snake, it will begin twirling and will keep up a constant movement, changing its direction from time to time.

## The Windmill Figure

The windmill figure operates on the same principle as the spinning snake, the only difference being that the convection currents are caused by the hot air rising above a lighted candle instead of above a radiator.

To build this toy, you need a sheet of thin metal foil, three pieces of thin stiff gardening wire about 1/16 inches in

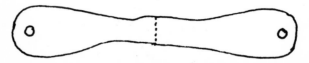

Figure 62. Arms for windmill figure. They are joined together, with dotted line where they will be folded.

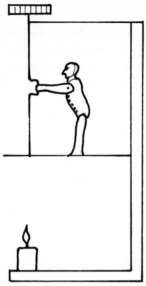

Figure 63. Windmill figure

diameter, one 8 inches, the other two 9 inches long, a 9-by-3-inch wooden board ½ inch thick, and 2 rivets about ½ inch long.

To make the figure itself, first draw the pieces for the figure on the sheet of foil. Draw the body and head in one piece, making it about 3 inches long and 1 inch wide at the waist. Draw the legs in one piece and the arms in one piece, with the hands attached to each other and the feet attached to each other, as shown in Figure 62. Make the arms 2½ inches long and the legs 2¾ inches long.

Cut the pieces out with your foil-cutting scissors. Fold the arms where the hands are joined, and the legs where the feet are joined. Using a bradawl or a leather-punching tool, make a rivet hole in the end of each limb and in the body where the limbs are to be joined to it. Now set the pieces for the figure aside while you make the framework for the toy.

Take two of the wires and with a round-pointed pair of pliers twist a loop at the end of each wire, making the loops

large enough for you to insert the third wire. Bend the center
of the third wire into a crank, shaping it like three sides of a
rectangle, as shown in Figure 63. Make the crank 1 inch long
and ½ inch wide. Use a square pair of pliers to do this.

Drill two ½-inch-deep holes, five inches apart, in the
wooden board, making them large enough for you to insert
a wire.

Take the two wires with the loops bent in them, insert the
unbent ends into the holes in the board, making sure the
loops are horizontal, and glue the wires into place with instant glue. Now insert the third wire through the loopholes
so that the bottom end extends just far enough below the loop
in the bottom wire for you to glue a plastic bead to the end
and the top end extends ½ inch above the upper loop. Then
glue a bead to the bottom end of the wire just below the loop.

Figure 64. Crookes' radiometer (professionally made version).

Slip another bead onto the top end, and glue it just above the loop.

When the glue is dry, turn the unit right side up and assemble the figure. To do this, wrap the hands around the inside of the crank and attach the arms to the body with the rivets. Then wrap the figure's feet around the bottom wire and attach the legs to the body the same way. To prevent the legs from slipping down so that the figure is sitting on the wire, take the pliers and bend the legs inward at the ankles.

Now to make the windmill. Cut a disk 3 inches in diameter out of the foil. Draw a concentric circle with a diameter of $\frac{1}{2}$ inch on this disk, and score 19 lines from this circle to the edge of the disk. These lines should be $\frac{1}{2}$ inch apart at the outer edge of the disk and almost meet at the inner circle. Using your foil-cutting scissors, cut along these lines up to the circle you have drawn.

When you have finished cutting along these lines, the windmill vanes will be all cut out. Twist each vane gently, so it is at an angle of about 45 degrees to its former position. A wooden letter opener will help you bend the vanes without wrinkling them or crumpling them up. Stick the windmill on the top end of the crank wire, so that it rests on the plastic bead, and glue it into position, using instant adhesive.

Place a lighted candle under the toy, making sure it is directly under the windmill. (See Figure 63, page 107.) As the convection current begins to move, the hot air will strike the vanes of the windmill, causing them to turn, and as the vanes turn, the figure will move up and down.

The Chinese use the same principle to make double lanterns with figures that revolve inside the outer shell of the lamp shade. These can often be seen in Chinatown, or in Chinese restaurants.

### Radiometer

The radiometer, which was invented by Sir William Crookes, consists of a glass bulb in which a partial vacuum has

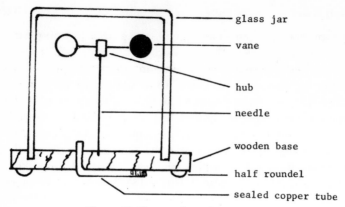

glass jar

vane

hub

needle

wooden base

half roundel

sealed copper tube

Figure 65. Homemade radiometer

been created and in which there are two crossed horizontal bars with vanes on the ends of them. These bars are supported in a way that enables them to rotate freely. One side of each vane is painted black; the other side is silver and polished. (See Figure 64.)

When the radiometer is placed in the sun, radiant energy coming from the sun is absorbed by the black surfaces, and thus the temperature of those surfaces is raised. The heated surfaces, in turn, heat the few remaining molecules of air near them, causing those molecules to move around more than the other molecules. (You have already learned that when air is heated, its molecules move apart.) As the molecules near the black surfaces become more active, the vanes start to revolve, and the speed with which they revolve indicates the intensity of the radiant energy.

It is because a partial vacuum has to be created inside the glass bulb that you will need the help of a science teacher, for you will have to use a vacuum pump to do this. If your school does not have one, perhaps your teacher will have access to one. In any case, you should ask your teacher to help you, since the jar could implode, or explode inward, when you use the pump.

The first step in making a radiometer is to acquire a stout glass jar with good clear glass. The glass must be thick and the jar should form a small dome. Try to get a jar about 6 inches tall and 4 inches in diameter. You will also need a 3-inch-long needle, a copper tube about 6 inches long and $\frac{1}{4}$ inch in diameter, some 1-inch-thick wood, two hardwood balls 1 inch in diameter, some light wood such as balsa, some aluminum foil, and some matte black enamel.

Make a base for the jar out of the 1-inch-thick wood. You can make either a round or a square base; but it should be an exact circle or square, and its diameter should be 1 inch greater than that of the jar. After you have cut out the base and sanded down the rough edges, place the mouth of the jar on the base, making sure the center of the jar is over the center of the base. (See Figure 65.) The jar will be properly positioned if the space between the jar and the edge of the base is the same on all four sides.

When the jar is in position, draw around its mouth with a sharp scriber. Then, using a gouge and a craft knife, cut a groove into the wood just inside this line. Make the groove wide enough to hold the rim of the jar and deep enough to sink the jar in for at least $\frac{1}{4}$ inch.

Next with a $\frac{1}{4}$-inch-gauge drill, drill a hole into *but not through* the center of the base. Make the hole about $\frac{1}{4}$ inch deep. Later you will insert the needle into it. To one side of the base's center, about 1 inch from it, drill another hole, large enough for you to insert the copper tube, all the way through the base.

Now make some legs for the base to stand on. To do this, put one of the hardwood balls in a vice, mark the center point, and cut it in two, trying to cut it into two equal halves. Do the same with the other ball. All the legs must be the same size, so the radiometer will balance properly. (You don't want it to wobble as a table sometimes does when one leg is shorter than the others.) If the legs are uneven, sand them down underneath to make them even. Glue the legs to the base with wood glue, placing them at the outer edge of the base as though they were at the ends of a cross. When the glue is dry, check to be sure the base stands firmly on a table. If not, sandpaper the legs some more until it does.

Take the copper tube, and 1 inch from one end, bend it so that it forms an angle that is as close to a right angle as you can make it. Use a vise to do this. Slip a plastic knitting needle in the tube when you bend it, or else you may close it. Insert the short end of the tube into the hole in the base, and glue it into place with rubber cement. The tube should extend for about 5 inches from the hole in the base, but because of the angle bent in it, it should not reach down below the legs and hit the table. (See Figure 65, page 110.)

Glue the needle, with the point sticking up, into the hole in the center of the base. Then make a hub to go on the end of the needle. The hub will hold the arms for the vanes. Use very light wood, such as balsa or the pith of an elder tree, that is $\frac{1}{2}$ inch thick, and with a craft knife cut out a disk $\frac{1}{2}$ inch in diameter. In the center drill a hole halfway through the hub, making the hole large enough so that when the needle is inserted in it, the hub will pivot on the needle.

Now with a craft knife cut out the four arms. You can make these out of the very thin split cane that small baskets are made of. (That is what I did when I made my radiometer.) With a jeweler's saw or a piercing saw, cut a slit about $\frac{1}{4}$ inch long in one end of each arm. After you have made the vanes, you will insert them into these slits. Cut the other end of each arm, so that it forms a point.

You will stick the pointed ends of the arms into the hub. So that you can do this, take a bradawl and make four tiny holes, just large enough to accept the arms, in the side of the hub. Place the holes so that the arms will stick out at right angles to each other and will be properly aligned. (You don't want some vanes to be higher than others.)

Figure 66

To make the vanes, cut four circles with a diameter of $\frac{1}{2}$ inch out of aluminum foil with your foil-cutting scissors. Paint one side of each vane with matte black enamel. When the enamel is dry, polish the other side gently with a cloth. Then insert the vanes into the slits in the arms, and glue them in place with contact cement.

When the glue is dry, glue the arms into the holes in the hub, inserting the arms so that the vanes are vertical and the blackened and polished sides alternate. If the black side of one vane faces the black side of the next vane, the radiometer will not work properly. Use balsa cement to glue the arms, and, if necessary, support them with putty so the vanes will align properly.

Again wait for the glue to dry, then gently place the hub on the end of the needle. Blow on the vanes to make sure they will spin around properly.

Polish the jar inside and out very thoroughly, then insert it in the groove in the wooden base, and glue it in place, using airtight cement. Now you have to use a vacuum pump to pump most of the air out of the glass jar.

To guard against the danger of flying glass if the jar should implode (shatter inwardly), while the air is being sucked out, cover the outside of the jar with transparent adhesive tape. Of course it is best if a laboratory technician or your teacher helps.

The possibility of implosion exists because of the force of the air pressure on the outside of the glass. Normally, when there is air inside the glass as well as outside, the outside pressure is counteracted by the pressure of the air inside the glass. In the 1650's a German scientist, Otto von Guericke, demonstrated the pressure of air by fitting together two hollow bronze hemispheres, which had a greased leather washer between them to help exclude the air. One of the hemispheres had a stopcock in it. The air was pumped out to create a vacuum, and then the stopcock was turned. Because of the air pressure outside the vacuum, the two hemispheres could not be separated until the air was let inside again. It is claimed that two teams of eight horses, each team harnessed to one of the hemispheres, could not pull them apart. Figure 66 shows two boys trying to separate two such spheres.

To pump the air out of your radiometer, couple the vacuum pump to the copper tube with a connecting link of rubber, then start the pump.

Once a partial vacuum is obtained, the vanes will begin to turn. At this point, compress about 1 inch of the copper tube with a pair of pliers and seal the end by forcing the walls of the copper together, being careful not to puncture the tube. Disengage the pump. Then seal the tube with airtight glue, such as thick rubber cement.

Take the adhesive tape off the jar, removing traces of adhesive with ether—be careful—ether is very inflammable. Make sure you don't upset the hub and shake it off its pivot. Place the radiometer in the sun, and it will go on turning as long as there is sunlight.

# 7. Weather and Climate Toys

The difference between weather and climate is that weather is concerned with conditions over a short period of time and climate is concerned with them over long periods of time. Weather is like a snapshot, climate like a movie.

Weather conditions include temperature, air pressure, wind, humidity, cloudiness, and precipitation at a given time. Climate is the average of these conditions over a long period. The major influence on an area's climate is its latitude, or its position on the earth. Near the equator, for instance, the climate is hot and humid with little change from season to season. Typical weather conditions would be hot and rainy.

In other areas, where there is more variation in the climate, the weather can be quite unpredictable. Even with modern scientific equipment, weather forecasting is not always accurate. The more information the scientist has, however, the more accurate his forecasts are.

The same is true when you use the weather-prediction toys discussed in this chapter. Their operation may be a little uncertain; when one of them is working perfectly, another may be going through a temperamental phase; or one may deliver its predictions after the weather change has already occurred; but if you make more than one of them, you can keep a record of how they operate, compare the predictions of one with those of another, and take more than one factor into account. The weather house, for instance, indicates the amount of humidity in the air, and the barometers indicate air pressure. In the chemical forecasters, the changes in a chemical solution are intended to indicate weather changes.

In addition to making these weather-prediction toys, you can make a Wardian case, in which a climate favorable to certain plants is maintained. And finally, you can make an outdoor windmill toy, which of course operates because of the wind—a factor in both weather and climate.

## Weather House

You are probably familiar with weather houses, such as the one in Figure 67, for although the toy was invented many

Figure 67. Weather house

years ago, it is still popular today. The figure dressed for rain emerges through the door when rain is expected, and the other figure, dressed for sunny weather, appears when it is not expected. Actually, the weather house is a type of hygrometer, which is an instrument that measures humidity, or the amount of water vapor in the air. Since a high degree of humidity can be an indication of rain, the weather house is used to predict whether or not rain is expected.

To make a weather house, first cut out the pieces for the cottage. Use ⅛-inch-thick hardboard. Make the front and back 3 inches wide, 4 inches high at the gable ends, and 6 inches high at the midpoint, where the two parts of the roof will come together. Make the sides 4 inches by 4 inches. Make the two parts of the roof 4½ inches by 4½ inches. Make the base 4 inches by 6½ inches. Cut all the pieces with a fretsaw or piercing saw, trying to keep all the cuts clean. Smooth down any rough edges with sandpaper.

Next cut the two doors and the round window out of the front. (See Figure 68.) Make the hole for the window 1¾

catgut

Figure 68. Weather house

inches in diameter, placing it midway between the two ends and level with the place where the wall begins to slope to accommodate the room. To cut the window out, drill a hole first, then use a piercing saw.

Make the doors ¾ inch wide and 3¾ inches high at the midpoint, rounding the top as in Figure 68. Place the doors ¾ inch from the ends with 1 inch between them. Cut ¼ inch away from the bottom of the piece between the doors. This will make room for the turntable on which the figures will stand. Save the two pieces of hardboard that you remove from the doors, and use them later to make the two figures.

To make the turntable, cut a disk 3 inches in diameter out of ⅛-inch-thick hardwood, and drill a hole in the center of it.

Glue four ½-inch-high and ½-inch-wide wooden dowels to the bottom of the base. Use wood glue and place one dowel in each corner of the base. These will serve as legs to raise the weather house slightly off the ground.

You can glue the back and side walls together, but leave the front to be put on later. When you glue the walls together, first take one of the side walls and glue two square wooden dowels to the inside edge. Then when the glue is dry, glue the back to the side wall and the dowels. This will help you to get good right angles at the corners. Glue the back to the other side wall in the same way.

When the walls are glued firmly, glue them onto the base. Again use dowels to make sure they are stuck at the right angle.

Before gluing the roof together, mark the midpoint on the edges that are to be glued together. Then take a file and make a groove on each edge so that when the two parts are glued together, there will be a hole large enough to admit a catgut string in the center of the roof.

Glue the two halves of the roof together, affixing them on top of the gable ends to make sure they stick together at the right angle. Then slip elastic bands over the roof to hold it to the house until it has stuck.

When the glue is dry, place the roof on top of the cottage, without gluing it. Mark its position on the side walls so you can glue it later in the same place. Tie a ring screw to a piece of thread, insert the thread through the hole in the roof, and fasten it with a piece of tape. The thread will serve as a plumb line and show you the spot on the floor that is directly beneath the hole in the roof. Mark this spot.

Then remove the roof and drill a hole in the floor at the spot you have marked. Make the hole just large enough for the catgut string. Then glue the roof onto the cottage. Leave the front off at this point. You can leave the plumb line attached to the roof while you do this to make sure the two holes are still aligned properly. When the glue is dry, remove the plumb line.

Take a piece of wire 3 inches long, bend it in a U shape and insert it through the hole in the turntable, so that it forms a loop above the turntable. Then attach the turntable to the floor of the cottage by pushing the two ends first through the hole in the turntable, then through the hole in the floor. Bend the ends of the wire outward. The turntable can now revolve freely on its wire axis.

Now paint the house with quick-drying paint. (You can paint the front, but leave it unattached.) You might paint the roof red and the walls blue, and paint a white rim around the doors and window of the front wall, or you can use some other color combination if you prefer.

When the paint is dry, take a thick catgut string, such as a banjo string (an 'F' string is a good thick one to use for this purpose), and knot it. Insert one end through the hole in the roof, and tie the other end to the wire loop above the turntable. Tie with a loop knot, because you will probably have to adjust the string later.

When there is water vapor in the air, the catgut will absorb the water vapor, and the moisture will cause it to twist and become shorter. When there is less water vapor in the air, the moisture will leave the catgut, causing it to untwist. As the catgut twists and untwists, it will cause the turntable to move, and after the figures have been placed on the turntable, they too will move.

Before you add the figures, let the weather house operate as it is for about a week, and watch the turntable to see how its position changes as the weather changes. This will enable you to determine where to place the figures so that the figure dressed in rainwear will come out through the door on humid days, and the other figure will emerge on dry days. Mark the positions as soon as you think you know where the figures should go. Then watch the turntable a few more days to make sure your markings are correct and adjust them if necessary.

Meanwhile you can make the figures. Take the two pieces of hardboard you saved for this, and draw the figures on them, putting a knob on the bottom of each foot. When the figures are attached to the turntable, these knobs will be inserted in holes in the turntable. Cut the figures out with a piercing saw and sandpaper the rough edges.

Paint the figures with quick-drying paint, and draw in the details, such as the faces, with a fine-nibbed pen, such as a mapping pen, and thinned-down paint. (You can also use the pen to draw details on the house, like the tiles on the roof.) Show the figure indicating bad weather with an umbrella, and when you paint him, dress him in a raincoat, perhaps a yellow slicker. Dress the other figure for fine weather. The man in Figure 68 is dressed for a game of cricket, but you may prefer to make him a yachtsman or baseball player.

When you are ready to add the figures to the weather house, slip a piece of wood between the turntable and the floor of the cottage to prevent the turntable from moving. Then, using a small auger, drill four holes in the turntable, putting them exactly where the figures' feet should go and making them large enough and just deep enough for the knobs on the figures' feet. Glue the figures in place with instant glue, then remove the wood from under the turntable.

You can also hang a piece of seaweed from the ceiling, positioning it so that it will hang inside the window. Seaweed also indicates the amount of humidity in the air. When it is humid, the seaweed feels moist; when the air is dry, the seaweed feels dry.

Now you can put the front on the weather house. However, the catgut may need adjusting, so don't glue the front on. You want to be able to reach the catgut so you can knot and retie it if necessary. Keep the front of the house loose so you can lift it off. When you do put it back, position four blocks of plastic putty inside the house. These will hold the front securely in place.

### Barometers

Barometers are instruments that measure air pressure, another factor in weather. When air pressure decreases rapidly, that is generally an indication that a storm is coming, and when it increases, fine weather is usually on the way.

### Homemade Water Barometer

In the first barometer, invented in 1643 by Evangelista Torricelli, the pressure of air on a column of water in a 34-foot tube was measured. Of course using a 34-foot tube is inconvenient, but you can make a much smaller weatherglass that operates on the same principle as Torricelli's instrument.

You need a flask or a bottle with a narrow neck, such as the one in Figure 69. In addition, you need a jar with a mouth that is just large enough for you to insert the flask or the neck of the bottle. Fill the jar with water. Then invert the flask and push its mouth down into the jar of water. The water will rise part of the way into the flask.

The air pressure pushing down on the water in the jar will

force some of the water to move up into the flask. The amount of water that will move up into the flask will depend on the air pressure. When the weather is fine, high pressure usually prevails. The water will rise farther in the flask, compressing the air that is above it. If it is likely to rain, low pressure predominates. The water level in the flask will go down.

## Mercury Barometer

Torricelli's instrument with its 34-foot tube was soon replaced by the mercury barometer. Since mercury is denser than water, an accurate mercury barometer can be made with a lot less mercury.

To make a mercury barometer, you need a test tube about 24 inches long, a Petri dish or bowl, and enough mercury to fill the tube and part of the bowl. Fill the tube with mercury and put the rest of the mercury in the saucer. Don't forget that mercury is extremely poisonous. Try to get your science teacher, who is used to handling toxic chemicals, to do the

Figure 69. Homemade water barometer

filling for you. It will make an interesting experiment for the class, so he or she will probably be glad to help you out. Then cover the mouth of the test tube with a piece of cardboard and turn the tube upside down, being careful not to let the mercury, which is heavy, break the cardboard. Lower the mouth of the tube onto the bottom of the saucer, and slowly pull out the cardboard.

Some of the mercury will move out of the tube into the saucer, leaving a vacuum in the space above the mercury. This vacuum is called the Torricellian vacuum. Since there is no air above the column of mercury in the tube, the mercury will be affected only by the pressure of the air on the mercury in the bowl, and that air pressure will keep the mercury from moving completely out of the tube. As with the home-made weatherglass, the level of the mercury will rise and fall as the air pressure increases and decreases.

In order to have a more accurate idea of how far the mercury has risen or fallen, you can make a paper scale and glue it to the outside of the tube. (See Figure 70.)

### Chemical Weather Forecasters

In the past people have tried to predict the weather by observing the changes in certain chemicals. Although the method is not entirely accurate, the instruments used are fun to experiment with. You should, however, ask a science teacher for help in mixing the chemicals. Don't forget many drug store proprietors are also interested in science and scientific toys. My local druggist was quite glad to mix up my forecaster.

### Chemical Weatherglass

The chemical weatherglass consists of a glass tube that contains a chemical solution and is mounted on a wooden frame. The solution in the tube becomes more or less cloudy as the weather changes.

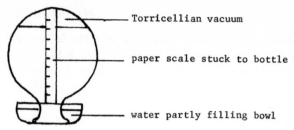

Torricellian vacuum

paper scale stuck to bottle

water partly filling bowl

Figure 70. Barometer with paper scale glued to it.

First buy your test tube, which should be 5 inches long and 1 inch in diameter. Then make the holder for it out of ½-inch-thick softwood, such as soft pine. The parts for the holder are shown in Figure 71. Using the dimensions given on the diagram, draw the parts on cardboard, cut them out; then use these parts as patterns to draw the parts on the wood.

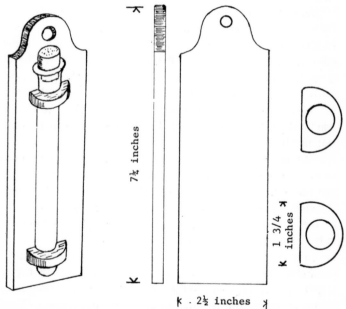

7¼ inches

1 3/4 inches

2½ inches

a  Completed Chemical       b  Parts for the Chemical
   Weatherglass                 Weatherglass

Figure 71. Chemical weatherglass

The holder should be 8 inches tall and 2½ inches wide. The holes in the brackets should be wide enough to hold your test tube. Stand the test tube on the brackets upside down and draw around it as a guide. The hole at the top should be ¼ inch wide.

Cut out the parts with a fretsaw, using a fine blade to ensure a clean cut, and rub down the pieces with fine sandpaper. Cut out the hole at the top of the holder with a twist drill.

Use a piercing saw to cut out the holes in the brackets. At each end of the back side of the brackets, drill a hole about ¼ inch deep. Push a headless nail into each hole, so that the point sticks out from the back of the bracket for about ¼ inch.

Mark the position for the brackets on the holder, placing them 4 inches apart and midway between the two sides of the holder. Cover the back side of one of the brackets with instant glue, and press it gently but firmly onto the holder. The wood should be soft enough so that you can push the points of the nails into the holder. Start the holes first by pushing them in with a bradawl. Fasten the second bracket in the same way. When the glue is hard, brush the holder with diluted polyurethane varnish.

Now ask a science teacher, or a druggist if you know one, to mix the chemicals in the solution. As I said my local druggist made up mine. Don't try to do this yourself, because the solution has to be heated, and absolute alcohol, which is one of the chemicals to be used, is extremely inflammable.

It is a good idea to make several weatherglasses at a time, because one is likely to be a better predicter than the rest.

The following quantities will give you enough of the solution to fill several weatherglasses: 2½ grams of camphor, 38 grams of potassium nitrate, 38 grams of ammonium chloride, 6 grams of absolute alcohol, and 9 grams of distilled water. If you want to make only one weatherglass, weigh the amount of water you can get into your test tube. Then add the total weight of all the materials I give (remembering 1 gram equals 0.0353 ounce). Divide the total by the weight of the contents of the test tube. This will give you the proportion by which the materials should be reduced.

When finished, put the tube in the holder. Then hang it someplace where it will not be affected by artificial heat, such as in a garage. As the weather changes, so will the nature of the solution. Sometimes the contents will crystallize, the extent of the crystallization depending on the weather. According to the predictions made in Victorian times, any change in the solid-to-liquid ratio means a change in the weather; fernlike crystals growing downward from the top mean cold and stormy weather; clear liquid means fine and warm weather; cloudy, thick liquid means wet weather; clearly defined fernlike crystals with sharp points mean very fine weather; and blunted, dispersing crystals mean unsettled weather.

I have found, however, that the weatherglasses in my garden studio react rather differently. Perhaps what you should do is to set up your own weatherglass, observe it, and keep a record of how it changes with changes in the weather.

## Chemical Barometer

To make a chemical barometer, obtain a test tube the size of the former, 5 inches high and 1 inch in diameter, and make another holder just like the one you made for the chemical weatherglass. Again ask a science teacher to help you. This time ask him to make a solution of 2 drams of pure niter, ½ dram of powdered chloride of ammonia, and 2 ounces of denatured alcohol, and to put it in your test tube. Use a cork to stop the top of the tube, but before inserting it in the tube, pierce it with a needle to make about 5 air holes in it.

After the barometer has stood long enough for the mixture

to settle down, the solution will react to changes in the weather. Theoretically, it should react as follows. If the weather is to be fine, the solid material will remain in the bottom of the tube, and the alcohol will be fairly clear. If it is going to rain soon, the alcohol will become cloudy, and some of the solid particles will rise and fall in it. And if a storm is coming in about twenty-four hours, the solid matter will rise to the surface of the alcohol and form a scum on it, and the alcohol will appear to be in a state of fermentation.

As with the chemical weatherglass, however, these predictions are not entirely reliable, and instead of depending on them, you should probably keep a record of how your chemical barometer reacts to changes in the weather.

## The Wardian Case

The Wardian case was invented in 1824 by Nathaniel B. Ward, who wanted to create an atmosphere in which his ferns would grow well. Ferns, popular plants in the nineteenth century, like a warm, humid climate and are sensitive to the noxious fumes found in city air. So Ward created a big glass box, which looked like a miniature greenhouse, where plants would live in their own separate atmosphere and thus the right climate could be maintained. (See Figure 72.)

In our own atmosphere, water, an important element in weather and climate, is continually moving through a cycle. When it falls as rain or snow, it sinks into the ground or settles in lakes, streams, or the oceans. Then it evaporates from the seas and other bodies of water or is taken from the ground through the roots of plants, used by the plants, and given off into the air through transpiration. Thus it moves from the ground back into the air, where it takes the form of water vapor, and when enough water vapor has accumulated in the air, it again falls to the ground.

Part of this cycle is reproduced in the Wardian case. Initially, when the garden in the Wardian case is created, the soil is well watered. Then after the case has been sealed, the water circulates inside it, just as the water circulates in a larger environment. It is taken up by the roots of the plants and, as the plants transpire, moves into the atmosphere. Then as it condenses on the inside of the glass, it moves down the glass back to the soil. Once the Wardian case has been set up, you can leave it to look after itself, without watering it.

Moreover, the enviroment remains both humid and warm—just the right climate for Ward's ferns. The atmosphere remains humid because the water vapor cannot escape. And the environment is warm because when the Wardian case is placed in the sunlight, the plants and soil absorb the radiant energy coming from the sun and then warm the enviroment through conduction and convection currents.

This too is similar to what happens in the earth's atmosphere. The earth absorbs radiant energy coming from the sun, and as areas of land are thus heated, the air above the land is heated. The air rises and a convection current is

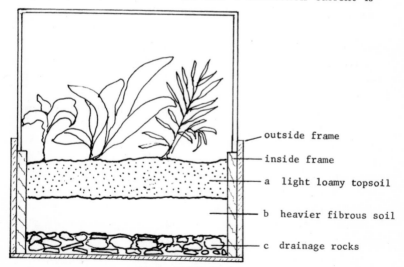

outside frame

inside frame

a   light loamy topsoil

b   heavier fibrous soil

c   drainage rocks

Figure 72. Wardian case

formed, just as it was when you made some of the heat toys discussed in Chapter 6. When this happens in the earth's atmosphere, the convection current causes clouds to form and thus rain to fall. When the heated air in the current strikes a layer of cooler air, the rising air is cooled to below its dew point—the temperature at which air at a certain pressure and with a certain amount of water vapor in it is saturated—and some of the excess moisture condenses to form clouds.

Thus when you make a Wardian case, you are creating a miniature environment with its own atmosphere. Today, instead of making a small greenhouse, you can make a Wardian case using a secondhand glass or plastic aquarium. If you find one that has a crack in it, you can probably buy it without paying very much, and you can seal the crack with a strip of adhesive tape and decorate the tape.

The aquarium will be covered with a glass lid. A half-inch strip of draft sealer—foam plastic with an adhesive backing—is stuck onto the underside of the lid, where it touches the walls of the aquarium, to keep out drafts.

Now you can add the soil and plants. Cover the bottom of the aquarium with a layer of drainage material—either the pieces of a broken clay flower pot or gravel. Then add a 2-inch layer of commercial potting soil and cover it with a layer of leaf mold.

Buy small plants for your Wardian case, and choose plants that grow well in warm, humid conditions. Ivies, such as English ivy *(Hedera helix)*, do well in Wardian cases. So do prayer plants *(Maranta leuconeura)*, baby's tears *(Helxine soleirollii)*, small-leaved figs and peperomias, and, although some are fragile, the Victorian favorite—ferns.

When you have added the plants, arranging them as artistically as you can, water the soil well, then place the lid on the aquarium. You may remove the lid from time to time to give the plants an airing, but do not water the plants again. Be careful not to place the Wardian case in a draft, and put it where the plants will get some sunlight, but not in direct, fierce sunlight.

## An Outdoor Windmill Toy

The windmill toy discussed in Chapter 6 operated because of convection currents, and convection currents do play a part in the weather, as indicated earlier. Outdoor windmills, however, operate because of air flowing parallel to the earth's surface, which is what wind is.

To make the windmill toy shown in Figure 73, cut the pieces out of thin, brightly colored plastic sheeting with a fretsaw. Make the base on which the figure will stand 2 feet long and 2 inches wide. Make the two end pieces for the frame that will hold the crank 5 inches long and 2 inches wide. Make the triangular-shaped piece at the end, which will act as a direction fan, with three angles, one of which is a right angle, and sides that are 3, 2, and 2¼ inches long.

Drill a hole for the crank wire in the exact center of each end of the frame. Cut a 1-inch slot in one end of the base for the direction fan, placing the groove in the exact center of the end. Drill a hole in the base 6 inches from the end where

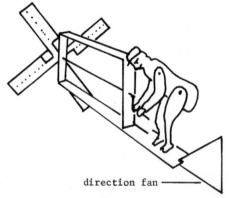

direction fan ────────

Figure 73. Windmill toy

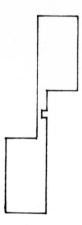

Figure 74. Each vane of the windmill is cut from plastic, then slotted together and cemented before being glued in the crosscut of the dowel hub.

the direction fan will be. Later you will insert a rod through this hole, and it will act as a pivot for the toy to revolve on. Then, 3 inches from where the direction fan will be, make two holes 7 inches apart. When you make the figure, you will put knobs on the bottom of its feet and insert these through the holes.

Using epoxy resin or the glue made especially for plastic, glue the four sides of the frame together, positioning the frame on the end of the base opposite the direction fan, as in Figure 73.

To make the crank, take a piece of stiff galvanized iron wire, and with a pair of pliers bend one end to form a crank shaped like the one in Figure 73. Stick the wire through the two holes in the frame for it.

To make the windmill, cut vanes out of plastic sheeting to the size and shape in Figure 74. Cement them, and slot them together. Leave them to dry.

Cut a 3-inch length from a wooden dowel 1 inch in diameter. Drill a hole, large enough to insert the wire in it, right through. At one end make two saw cuts with a wood saw, which intersect one another in a cross whose arms are at right angles to one another. Enlarge the saw cuts with a file

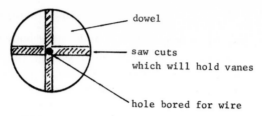

Figure 75. Dowel bored and sawn to hold vanes for windmill.

until they are big enough to hold the two vanes. (See Figures 75 and 76.)

Stick the vanes into the dowel with contact cement. Stick the wire into the hole drilled in the other end of the dowel. The dowel should be clear of the framework so that it is able to rotate freely. Insert the crank wire into the hole in the dowel, and glue the dowel in place.

Now cut the pieces for the figure out of plastic. Cut out the head and body in one piece, making it 5 inches long and about 1½ inches wide at the waist. Cut the arms out, making them 3 inches long including the hands. Make the legs 4 inches long. Cut them out as two separate pieces also and be sure to put knobs on the bottom of the feet, making the knobs the right size for insertion into the holes in the base.

Drill a hole in each hand, making the holes large enough for you to insert the crank wire through them. Drill rivet

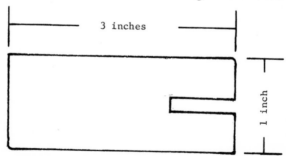

Figure 76. Dowel to hold vanes seen in side view.

holes at the top of the arms and legs and in the body where the limbs are to be attached. Put the pieces of the figure together, fastening them with rivets.

Then slip the crank wire through the holes in the figure's hands. Push the knobs on the feet into the holes in the base, and glue them in place. When the figure is in position, slip the direction fan into the groove for it and cement it in place.

Now you can mount the toy on a wooden pole. To do this, drill a hole in the top of the pole, making the hole large enough for you to insert the rod you are using for a pivot. A solid plastic ball, drilled through, is stuck to the rod so that the frame of the windmill toy can rest on it and rotate freely. Stick the pole into the ground, insert the pivot through the hole in the base and into the hole in the pole. As soon as there is a breeze, the windmill will begin turning.

# 8. Chemical Toys

When certain chemicals come in contact with each other, they undergo a chemical reaction. Or when they are subjected to changes in pressure or are heated to specific temperatures, they may undergo a chemical reaction. In any chemical reaction, at least one substance is changed to one or more new substances. A simple example is the decomposition of water. One molecule of water is made of two atoms of hydrogen and one atom of oxygen. When water is decomposed, the hydrogen atoms form hydrogen molecules, and the oxygen atoms form oxygen molecules, so that the water changes to hydrogen and oxygen.

Most chemical reactions are much more complicated than that, however. The exact circumstances under which a chemical reaction occurs depend on what chemicals are involved, as does the nature of the reaction itself. Some chemical reactions are accompanied by color changes; others involve changes from liquid to solid states; and sometimes a change to the solid state involves a color change as well.

By using the right chemicals, you can paint a magic landscape in which the foliage changes color because the chemicals themselves change color. And by combining the right chemicals, you can make a variety of crystals and use them to create trees, gardens, or jewelry.

Chemicals, however, are not something to play with. When you make the following toys, enlist your father's or some other adult's help. Be sure to follow the directions carefully, and do not mix other chemicals unless you have specific instructions for doing so. If you mix chemicals at random, you could very well have a reaction you don't want, such as an explosion. Make sure your chemicals are pure; explain to your druggist just what you want them for.

Buy utensils especially for making these toys and use them *only* for that. Do not let them get mixed up with the household utensils, and keep them out of the kitchen sink. Lead, for instance, is poisonous. So be sure none of the utensils or the chemicals are left where a younger brother or sister can get hold of them or where someone else might use them by mistake.

## Magic Landscape

The magic landscape, which was popular with children a hundred years ago, is a painting that changes with the seasons. In the winter the trees and fields appear to be covered with snow, and in the summer they appear to be green and verdant. That is because the painting is done with chemicals that change color when they are exposed to the heat of the sun.

To make a magic landscape, take some white paper, and paint the outlines of the trees, roads, buildings, and fences in India ink, which will not change. Then make a copper sulfate solution. To do this, dissolve as much copper sulphate in a solution of water as it will take before reaching saturation point—that is, until the water holds as much copper sulfate as it can without having the copper sulfate sink to the bottom. Use this solution to paint the trunks and branches of the trees as well as the buildings and fences.

Then make a strong solution of chloride of cobalt and nickel, and dilute it with distilled water sufficiently so that it will flow freely. Use it to paint the meadows and the leaves of the trees.

Since heat is what causes these chemicals to change, you

have to hang the picture in a heated or unheated area for the right effect. In the winter, hang the picture in an unheated room, and the chemicals will appear white, giving the effect of a snow-covered landscape. In the summer, hang the picture by a window where the sun will strike it, and the chemicals will change color, the trunks of the trees and the buildings turning brown and the foliage turning green.

## Crystal Toys

Under the right conditions, the chemicals in a solution will form solid particles called crystals. Crystals are solids in which the atoms, molecules, or ions are held together in a definite, orderly shape as a result of chemical reactions. Solids that are composed of crystals are said to have a crystalline structure, and most solids are crystalline, but not all of them.

Wood, for instance, which comes from living trees, has a cellular structure, or is composed of cells. In general, however, inorganic solids, or solids that did not originate with plants or animals, are crystalline. A diamond, for example, is a crystal, and so are sugar and table salt. The substances making up rocks can only be crystallized with special equipment, but many others can be crystallized quite easily, as you will see.

## Iron Crystal Tree

To make an iron crystal tree, take a glass beaker and half fill it with nitric acid. Dissolve iron filings in the acid until it is saturated. Pour in oil of tartar until the solution begins to effervesce and throw up plantlike crystals. Tendrils of crystals will escape from the main mass and climb over the sides of the beaker.

## Lead Crystal Tree

Before making the chemical solution for the lead crystal tree, obtain a bottle, such as an acid bottle, that is made of thick glass and is stopped with a cork, some thin copper or brass wire, and some zinc. You can obtain the wire by un-twisting some light cable and soldering it to a slug of zinc, a sizable piece about as large as a lump of sugar. Take the wire and bend it so it is shaped like a little tree, making it small enough to fit in the bottle without touching the glass. Bend short pieces of wire so that they look like tree branches and twist them onto the stems.

With an auger make a hole in the center of the cork. Then tie a thin thread to the top of the wire tree. Stick the other end of the thread through the hole in the cork and fasten it to the top of the cork. Make the thread just long enough for the tree and its zinc base to dangle inside the bottle without touching the glass.

Now you are ready to make the solution. To as much as will fill the bottle of distilled water or rainwater, add ½ ounce of powdered sugar of lead and 10 drops of nitric acid, or the same amount of vinegar. Then clean the glass bottle and add the solution to it, making sure there is enough solution in the bottle so the tree will not protrude from the solution.

Insert the tree through the mouth of the bottle, and let it dangle on the end of the thread. With time, sparkling silvery-gray lead crystals will begin to deposit on the branches of the tree, giving it the appearance of being covered with hoarfrost.

## Sugar Candy Trees

For the sugar candy trees, instead of making a small tree out of wire, use some straw, or small twigs, perhaps some fibers that are forked so they form a natural treelike shape. Make a strong solution of white granulated sugar and water by boiling a cupful of sugar in ½ pint of water until the solution is thick. Pour the solution into a jar.

Tie the straw to a piece of thread. Tie the other end of the thread to a piece of wire, and lay the wire across the mouth of the jar so that the straw dangles in the sugar solution. As the sugar cools, it will crystallize around the branches of the tree.

You can make another tree in the same way using a solution of molasses and water. For this solution boil the same amount of molasses in ½ pint of water.

## Colored Crystal Trees

You can also use straw to make a tree coated with alum crystals. For your solution add alum to half a pint of distilled water until the solution is almost saturated. Half a pint of water should hold about a cup full of alum. Then add food coloring, which you can buy in various colors. Ink can be used for black and blue.

Heat this solution in a heat-proof beaker to 5 degrees above room temperature.

When the solution has been heated to the proper temperature, pour it into the beaker and dangle a piece of straw in it, in the same way that you dangled the straw in the sugar solution. Leave the straw in the solution for a day or so, until crystals begin to form on the branches. Then remove the tree, put the solution back in a jar, and boil the alum solution so as to make it stronger. When the solution begins to look thick and opaque, hang the straw tree in it again.

You can use this procedure also to make a tree of copper sulfate crystals, which are a brilliant blue. For this solution use about a third of a beakerful of copper sulfate and enough distilled water to reach the top of the beaker. Stir and let all the copper sulphate become dissolved.

Again dangle the straw in the solution until crystals begin to form; then remove the tree, boil down the solution to make it stronger, and return the tree.

When you have a collection of little trees, you can anchor them in a decorative dish with a little tacky putty. Then you can create a landscape by breaking up your extra sugar, copper sulfate, or alum crystals and placing them around the trees, perhaps forming mountains with some of the larger crystals.

## Crystal Jewelry

If you liked one kind of crystal tree better than the others, you can make some jewelry out of the same kind of crystals. Don't use lead crystals because skin contact with lead could be poisonous. Make some more of the solution that you used for the tree, and produce from it a few small crystals. They will form by themselves. Remove these with tweezers. Boil the solution so as to make it stronger; then put the small crystals in the stronger solution, leaving them there until they grow larger.

When you have several crystals of a matched size, remove them from the solution, and let them dry out thoroughly. Do not heat them in order to dry them, because that would alter their color. You can, however, varnish them, preferably by spraying.

From a craft shop buy jeweler's findings to fit your crystals. You can buy findings for earrings, cuff links, or if you have one crystal you like particularly, a tie tack. Glue the crystals to the findings with epoxy resin. If you want to make a necklace, buy bell caps and jump-ring findings. Then glue these to the crystals and string them together.

Or you can make a rather spiky necklace of small crystals by taking a long human hair or horse's hair, washing it well with detergent to remove any grease, and dunking it in the solution until crystals have grown on it. You would have to buy only the clasp for this necklace.

## Crystal Garden

You can make a crystal garden in any kind of clear glass container, such as an old aquarium, a goldfish bowl, a preserving jar, an old acid carboy, or a decorative glass bottle. Wash the container and determine how much solution you will need. To do this, fill the container with water until the water level is 3 inches from the top of the container. Then pour the water into a quart measure or some other measuring jug and note the quantity.

Cover the bottom of the container with a 2-inch layer of washed sand and scatter some lumps of copper sulfate, a few pieces of aluminum, and some iron nails on the sand.

Now mix up the solution using whatever amount of water you poured into the quart measure. Make a solution that is three parts distilled water to one part sodium silicate. In other words, if you use 3 cups of distilled water, use 1 cup of sodium silicate; if you use 6 cups of distilled water, use 2 cups of sodium silicate, etc.

Using a long funnel, so as not to disturb the layer of sand, pour the solution gently into the container, and let it stand for a few days. The silica in the sodium silicate will combine with the copper sulfate, the aluminum, and the iron, and beautifully colored silica growths will begin to appear. When these growths are fully formed, siphon off the sodium silicate solution and replace it with clear water, dribbling the water onto the bottom of the container through a rubber tube so as not to damage the delicate crystals.

If you want to give this crystal garden a special touch, you can make a summer house covered with blue copper sulfate crystals. To do this, fasten together some straw fibers with contact cement so that they form the frame of a house. You can also use thread covered wire. Use the solution you used for the copper sulfate tree and the same procedure for forming the crystals on the house that you did for forming the crystals on the tree. When the summer house is finished, place it on an open space between the crystal plants.

# 9. Electric Toys

During the infancy of electrical science, before current electricity was developed, demonstrations of static electricity were a favorite form of amusement, and many of the toys discussed in this chapter were developed for such entertainment. Nevertheless, these toys, all of which are powered by static electricity, do demonstrate some of the principles of electricity.

Static electricity was noticed as long ago as 600 B.C. by the ancient Greeks, who discovered that if they rubbed amber with a piece of cloth, it would pick up bits of fluff, dust, or straw. Centuries later scientists realized that when the amber was rubbed with the fabric, it became electrically charged because of the friction between the amber and the cloth. When the particles stuck to the amber, the stone was exhibiting what we now call electrical attraction.

In the 1700's scientists realized there are two kinds of electricity, which Benjamin Franklin named negative and positive electricity, and it is because of these two kinds of electricity that substances exhibit electrical attraction. When two substances are oppositely charged, they attract each other. That is, a negative charge and a positive charge attract each other. Two negative charges, however, repel each other.

When glass, sealing wax, and certain other substances are rubbed with flannel or fur, they become negatively charged. If, however, glass is rubbed with silk, the glass becomes positively charged.

Materials such as glass and sealing wax, which can thus be charged through friction, are called insulators because they retain the electric charges instead of passing them on to some other substance. Some substances, such as metal, do pass electric charges on, and they are called conductors, for they conduct the electricity from one place to another. These substances cannot be charged by rubbing and are difficult to charge at all if they are not insulated. They are used, however, to conduct a current of electricity through an electric circuit.

You can begin making electric toys with some simple toys, such as the electric boxers. which require no more electricity than that which you can generate by rubbing sealing wax or glass. Then you can go on to make an electrophorus, an instrument that will generate electric charges, and a Leyden jar, a device that will store the electric charges. Using the electrophorus to charge the Leyden jar, you can then use the jar to operate numerous toys, such as the dancing dolls, and even to create imitation thunderclouds.

## Electric Boxers

To make electric boxers, take a piece of thin cardboard and glue a sheet of aluminum foil to one side of it. Draw two

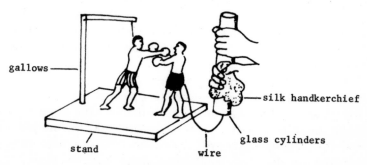

Figure 77. Electric boxers

small boxers, about 6 inches high, on the other side of the cardboard, and cut the boxers out.

Take a wooden board about 10 inches by 2 inches, and attach a wooden gallows, like the one shown in Figure 77, to the board. To do this, cut an upright from a wood dowel, ½ inch thick and 9 inches high. Drill a hole to take this in the baseboard, two inches in from the end. Cut an upright from a strip of wood 4 inches long and ½ inch wide and ⅛ inch thick. Drill a hole through one end of it, saw a groove on top of the upright and glue it in place.

With a needle make a hole in the top of the head of one of the boxers; insert a cotton thread through the hole and, using the thread, suspend the boxer from the gallows. Stand the other boxer upright on the wooden board with a dab of sealing wax so that he is almost in contact with the first boxer but not quite. With adhesive tape attach a thin piece of fuse wire to the aluminum side of the upright boxer. This will act as a conducter and carry the electric charge to the boxer.

Now to make a generator for your boxers. For this, obtain a glass chimney, such as those used in old kerosine lamps or in modern electrified versions of them. Warm and dry the glass by placing it on a hot radiator. It is important to dry the glass in this way because any water vapor in the air will tend to adhere to the glass, and since water vaper is a partial conductor of electricity, it will make charging the glass difficult. In fact, this and the following electric toys will work better in the winter than in the summer because the air is generally drier in the winter.

When the glass chimney is warm and dry, rub it vigorously with a silk handkerchief, or some other piece of silk cloth, and the glass will discharge small quantities of static electricity. Place the chimney so that it is in contact with the fuse wire, and the hanging boxer will rush at the standing one, then retreat hurriedly, then lunge again at the standing boxer.

As long as there is static electricity in the lamp chimney,

the suspended boxer will continue to lunge at and withdraw from the standing boxer. That is because the static electricity in the glass chimney passes through the fuse wire and charges the standing boxer. When the hanging boxer lunges at him, the standing boxer imparts some of his charge to his opponent. Since like charges repel each other, the hanging boxer is repelled as soon as he receives the electric charge and thus retreats from the standing boxer. He soon loses the charge, however, through the cotton thread. He is then attracted to his opponent, lunges at him again, and is again charged and thus repelled by his opponent. And so it goes on.

## Jumping or Swinging Pith Balls

You can use the same principle to cause balls of pith from an elder branch to jump about. Or if you cannot obtain elder pith, you can force balls carved from balsa wood to hop about. Make them about ¼ inch in diameter.

Place your pith balls or balsa balls on a bench. Then charge a piece of sealing wax with static electricity by rubbing it on flannel. Hold the sealing wax out to the pith balls or balsa chips, and they will quickly jump up and down. Like the suspended boxer, they are first attracted to the sealing wax, then, as they are charged by the wax, repelled by it; then, as they lose their charge to the bench, they are again attracted to the wax, and so on until the wax has lost most of its charge.

As a variation of this trick, you can tie a silk thread around a pith ball and suspend it from a gallows like the one you made for the electric boxers. Again charge the sealing wax by rubbing it on flannel. Then hold it out to the ball. The ball will first swing toward it and then swing back.

## Electroscope

An electroscope is an instrument that detects the presence of electricity. The pith ball acts as a kind of electroscope, for its movements indicate the presence of electricity.

revolving pointer                              top piece

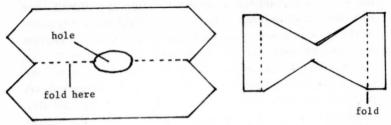

hole

fold here

fold

Figure 78. Make up the paper electroscope from two paper sections exactly these sizes.

You can make another electroscope out of a piece of cork, a straight pin, and some paper. To do this, cut a flat section, about ½ inch thick, from a large cork. Take the pin and with pliers snip off the head. Then, using a pair of pliers, force the end of the pin where the head was into the cork so that the point of the pin sticks up from the cork.

Now make a revolving pointer like the one shown in Figure 78. Do this by taking two pieces of paper, the sizes and shapes shown in the illustration. Mount the pointer on the end of the pin. Just let it balance on it.

When the electroscope is placed in the presence of electricity, the pointer will revolve like a compass needle. (See

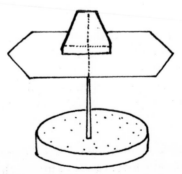

Figure 79. Electroscope on stand

Figure 79.) To demonstrate, take a glass rod, warm and dry it by placing it on a hot radiator, rub it with a dry silk handkerchief, and hold it near the electroscope. The pointer will point towards the rod. Or you can place the electroscope under an inverted tumbler and rub one side of the glass with a dry silk handkerchief. The pointer will turn toward the side you have rubbed.

## Waltzing, Swinging, and Walking Figures

You can make numerous figures out of paper and use static electricity to make them move. Waltzing figures are a good example. To make these, draw a man and a woman on brightly colored tissue paper and cut them out. Very tiny figures work the best, so don't make them any taller than ¾ inch. After you have cut them out, you can either have them stand separately or paste the hands of two figures together so they form a couple.

Place the figures on a table, and put a book at least 2 inches thick on each side of them. Then lay a sheet of glass on the books. Take a silk handkerchief, warm it, and rub the glass vigorously. The figures will be attracted by the static electricity and begin to jump up and down.

You can also make a swinging figure. To do this, make a paper framework, 3 inches by 3 inches, by cutting out four strips of thin cardboard, ½ inch wide, and taping them together to form a rectangle. Cut the seat of a swing out of paper, making it about ½ inch long and ¼ inch wide, and suspend it from the framework with two fine threads. Cut a minute man, no more than ¾ inch tall, out of paper and paste him to the seat of the swing. Electrify some sealing wax by rubbing it on flannel, and hold it out toward the man. Once he receives a charge, he will become a magnet that repels the sealing wax.

And you can use electrified sealing wax to make a paper figure walk about. Make a very small paper figure, no more than ¾ inches tall, and bend its feet over so it can stand.

Electrify the sealing wax and hold it out toward the figure. The figure will move toward the wax and follow it about.

## Self-Adhesive Writing Paper and Electric Wallpaper

To make self-adhesive writing paper, warm a sheet of stationery by placing it on a radiator, and lay it flat on a clean wooden table. Clench your fist and rub it over the paper. Soon the static electricity will cause the paper to stick to the table so it won't slide about. If you raise one corner of the paper slightly, the electricity will cause it to jump back.

Brown paper generates a high electric charge when rubbed with a brush or on one's clothing, and it can be electrified so that it will stick to the wall. To make this electric wallpaper, get some brown paper that has not been creased or wrinkled, and cut a piece that is no larger than 4 inches by 3 feet. Hold the paper near the radiator until it is dry and hot, or dry it in an oven set at 150 degrees for a few minutes.

Put on a long-sleeved shirt or sweater, then place the paper under your arm and press your arm against your side. Draw the paper briskly back and forth, so that it is being rubbed on both sides by the fabric. Place it against the wall and hold it there. After a few minutes it will stick to the wall for a short while without falling. If the paper is highly charged, you can make a light, fleecy feather adhere to it by placing the feather near the paper.

You can also demonstrate the paper's electric charge with a pith ball. Warm up and electrify the paper as before. Then lay it on a table, and place a pith ball about the size of a pea on it. The ball will immediately roll across the paper.

## Flying Feather

Not only will a light, fleecy feather adhere to highly charged electric wallpaper, but you can also make a feather fly around the room. To do this, warm a wineglass or a glass rod, charge it by rubbing it with a silk handkerchief, and bring it near

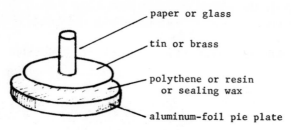

paper or glass

tin or brass

polythene or resin
or sealing wax

aluminum-foil pie plate

Figure 80. Electrophorus

a downy feather. At first the feather will adhere to the glass, but as soon as it has been charged by the glass, it will fly from the glass. And if you hold the glass between the feather and the other objects in the room, you will be able to drive the feather around the room. If, however, the feather touches something in the room that causes it to lose its electric charge, it will immediately fly back to the glass rod.

## Swinging Pipe

You can also use static electricity to get a pipe to swing around. Get a long-stemmed clay pipe, and lay it across the top of a water glass, so that the pipe can revolve freely. Warm and dry a silk handkerchief by placing it on a radiator and rub a clean wineglass with it. Hold the wineglass near the end of the pipe. The mouthpiece will be attracted by the electricity, and if you move the wineglass around the water glass, the pipe will revolve as the mouthpiece follows the wineglass.

## Electrophorus

If you make an electrophorus, you will be able to generate more static electricity than you can with a glass rod or a piece of sealing wax, for the electrophorus is an instrument that produces electric charges. As you can see from Figure 80, it consists of two disks, one of which has a handle attached to it.

Figure 81

Thus your first step in making the instrument is to obtain the two disks. The top one should be 7 inches in diameter, and if possible, it should be made of thin brass, copper, or zinc. If you have trouble obtaining a disk of one of these materials, however, you can make a disk by cutting one out of ½-inch-thick wood and covering it with aluminum foil.

Make the bottom disk out of a cookie tin and make it 8 inches in diameter. Glue a circle of polythene, which is plastic made from polyethylene, or of alkathene to the top of this disk. You can obtain the polythene by buying a cheap dish and cutting out the bottom, but make sure the dish is made of the right kind of plastic.

Or if you prefer, you can make the bottom disk of sealing wax, which is what children did a hundred years ago. Take a circular pie plate made of metal foil, the kind store-bought pies come in, and fill it with pieces of broken sealing wax. Place the pie plate on an asbestos mat on a hot plate or an electric stove, and leave it there until the wax melts and fills the pie plate to a depth of at least ½ inch. When the wax has melted, remove the plate from the heat and place it on a flat surface, leaving it there until the wax has cooled and hardened. Once the wax is hard, remove the pie plate by cutting down to the top of the wax disk with a sharp craft knife and then tearing away the foil.

Make a handle out of a wood dowel ½ inch thick and attach it to the top disk with impact cement.

Now you can use the electrophorus to produce electric charges. Separate the two disks and rub the bottom one vigorously with fur, warm wool, flannel, or even nylon. (In Victorian times children used a cat skin, but you might find that a bit difficult to obtain.) After you have rubbed the bottom disk, it will be negatively charged. Take the top disk by the handle and place it on the bottom disk. As a result of the contact, the upper surface of the top disk will be positively charged, and the bottom surface will be negatively charged. Touch the top disk for a moment with your forefinger, and the negative charge, which is repelled by the negatively charged bottom disk, will be conducted away. Taking it by the handle, lift the top disk, and it will now be positively charged, so that you can draw a spark from it.

Be sure when you use the electrophorus that you are not near something inflammable. If a spark should be drawn in the presence of a combustible gas, it could cause an explosion. The boy in Figure 81 is intentionally using an electrophorus to set off an explosive charge of hydrogen and oxygen in order to fire a cork from a Victorian toy called Volta's cannon. The toy is rather dangerous, however, and thus not one that you should play with.

You could, however, use the electrophorus to light a candle, which should prove that there is a fire hazard if you are not careful. First light a candle with a match, then blow it out. You can ignite it again with a spark from the electrophorus by holding the charged disk to it.

Figure 82. Leyden jar

You can also use the electrophorus to do some simple tricks such as the next one.

### Jumping Frogs

To make jumping frogs, draw some very small frogs, about ¾ inch long, on green tissue paper and cut them out. Wet a piece of blotting paper and moisten the frogs slightly by dabbing them with the blotting paper. Rub the bottom disk with flannel. Put the top disk on the electrophorus and lay the frogs on it. Touch the disk with your finger, then raise it by the handle, and the frogs will jump off onto the table.

### Leyden Jar

The electrophorus can also be used to charge a Leyden jar. A device used to store electric charges, the Leyden jar can be constructed from a glass conserve or pickle jar, as shown in Figure 82.

To make a Leyden jar, line the bottom two thirds of the

conserve jar with aluminum foil. To do this, first cut out a circular piece of foil that is a little larger than the bottom of the jar. Cover one side of the circle with cold water paste and press the foil down onto the inside bottom of the jar, running your finger over the foil so that it takes the shape of the jar.

Now cut a strip of foil that is large enough to cover the bottom two thirds of the sides of the jar, with the foil overlapping slightly at the edges. Glue the foil inside the jar with bookbinder's paste or PVA adhesive. Smooth the foil with your finger or with a plastic knife handle when necessary. Cover the bottom two thirds of the outside of the jar in the same way.

To make a cover for the Leyden jar, take a piece of wood and cut out a disk the same size as the mouth of the jar. You now need a brass rod with a knob at one end and a brass chain at the other end. Brass chains and knobs can often be obtained from out-of-date light hangings or stairs. Drill a hole through the center of the wooden top, making the hole the same size as the brass rod, and insert the rod through the hole. Make sure the rod is inserted far enough so the brass chain touches the aluminum foil on the bottom of the jar.

Now you can charge the Leyden jar. Be careful when you handle the jar, however, for once it is charged you could get a slight shock from it. Before picking it up, always touch the outside with your forefinger. This will remove the outside charge.

Before charging the jar, make sure the top disk of the electrophorus is positively charged, following the instructions on page 151. Then hold the disk near the brass knob on the cover of the Leyden jar, and let the knob take fifty to a hundred sparks from it. The electricity will pass through the brass, which acts as a conductor, into the jar.

Once the Leyden jar is charged, you can use it to operate several toys, a few of which follow.

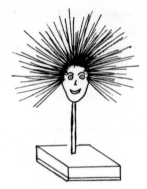

Figure 83. The electrified wig

### The Electrified Wig

If you can find one, buy a doll's head with long hair. If not, buy a cheap wooden doll with long hair and cut off its head, or if you prefer, you can carve a head out of wood and glue a wig onto it.

Make a wooden stand from a piece of softwood 3 inches square and 1 inch deep. Drill a hole $\frac{1}{8}$ inch wide right in the center. Glue a piece of stiff wire $\frac{1}{8}$ inch thick and 5 inches long into the stand. Glue a piece of rubber to the bottom of the stand to insulate it.

When the head is completed, touch the wire with the Leyden jar, and the hair on the head will stand on end, just as it does in Figure 83.

### Dancing Dolls

Just as you made figures move about with electrified sealing wax or with glass that had been rubbed with silk, you can use the Leyden jar to make figures dance about. Draw some very small dancing figures, no more than $\frac{1}{2}$ inch tall, on pith or balsa wood, and cut them out with a piercing saw. Place the figures under an inverted wineglass, touch the bottom of the glass with the knob of the Leyden jar, and the figures will jump up and down.

If you have a brass plate, you can use that to carry out the same trick. Place the plate an inch or so above the figures. Attach the plate to the knob of the Leyden jar. Again the figures will jump up and down.

### Imitation Thunderclouds

To make imitation thunderclouds, complete with a bolt of lightning, first make a wooden stand like the one shown in Figure 84. Cut the parts out of ½-inch-thick wood, making the base of the stand 12 inches by 6 inches, and the upright pieces at the ends 5 inches by ½ inch. Glue the upright pieces to the base with wood glue.

Cut two imitation clouds out of cardboard and cover them with aluminum foil, gluing the foil onto the cardboard with PVA.

Take two pieces of silk thread, several inches long, and suspend them from the two uprights on the wooden stand. Attach the two clouds by two plastic curtain rings, glued to the clouds with PVA, through which rings the fixed thread passes. The fixed wires pass through holes in the uprights.

Glue a brass ball to each cloud, placing the balls at the ends of the clouds that are nearest to each other.

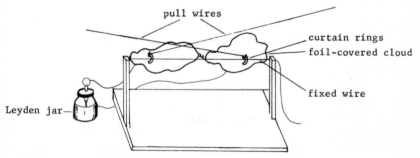

Figure 84. Lightning flash between clouds

Attach a wire to each cloud. Run the wire from one cloud to the brass knob on the Leyden jar, and run the other wire to the aluminum foil on the outside of the jar.

Now start the clouds at the opposite ends of the silk threads, and using the pull strings, pull them slowly toward each other until they are about an inch apart. At that point a bright flash, resembling a miniature thunderbolt, will pass from one cloud to the other.

### Lightning That Strikes

Instead of creating a flash of lightning that passes between imitation clouds, you can create a bolt of lightning that strikes a model ship or house. To do so, make another wooden stand like the one you just made, and suspend one thundercloud, also made of cardboard covered with aluminum foil, in the same way you suspended the other clouds.

Paint the base of the stand blue to make it resemble a sea, painting it with waves flecked with white if you wish. Draw the hull of a sailing ship on some thin cardboard, and cut it out. Make a mast, such as the one shown in Figure 85, out of thin split cane and glue it to the hull. Use some thread for rigging. Or, if you want to, you can make the rigging by running fine lengths of balsa cement out from the side of the spars, letting the cement harden, and then painting it.

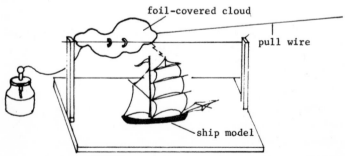

Figure 85. Lightning striking ship

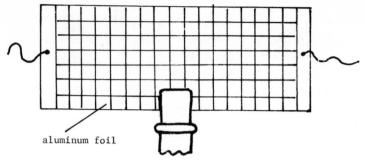

aluminum foil

Figure 86. Lightning board

Place the ship on the blue base of the wooden stand. Then run a fine wire from the cloud to the knob of the Leyden jar. Run another wire from the base of the mast to the aluminum foil on the outside of the jar.

Then draw the cloud slowly along the thread until it overhangs the ship. As it passes over the ship, the mast will be struck by a miniature flash of lightning and shattered to pieces.

If you prefer to have a model house instead of a ship struck by lightning, cut the pieces for a boxlike house with a flat roof out of cardboard and paint them. (You could also paint the base of the stand green instead of blue so it will resemble a lawn.) Lean the pieces together so that they form a house; don't bother to fasten them. Stick a small brass ball to the roof and surround it with four small pieces of cardboard so it looks like a chimney. Run a wire from the brass ball to the foil on the outside of the Leyden jar, and another wire from the cloud to the knob of the jar, as before. When you pull the cloud over the house, a miniature flash of lightning will dart toward the small brass ball, and the house will collapse.

## Lightning Board

To make a lightning board, take a sheet of thin glass and wash it thoroughly. Then mix some powdered sealing wax with denatured alcohol and brush the mixture over the sheet of glass on one side. Press a sheet of aluminum foil onto it.

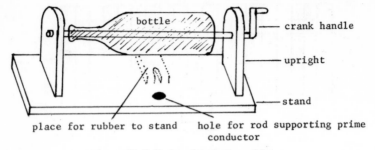

Figure 87. Cylinder electrical machine

Rub the foil down and allow it to dry. When the aluminum foil has dried out, take a craft knife and, using a straight edge as a guide, cut squares in the foil, leaving a solid strip of foil at each end, as shown in Figure 86.

To mount the glass, take the cork from a bottle and using a cabinet saw cut a slot in the top of it, making the slot just large enough for you to insert the glass. Glue the sheet of glass into the slot.

Attach a wire to the solid strip of foil at each end of the sheet, fastening it with a piece of tape. Take the lightning board and your Leyden jar outdoors and connect one of the wires to the knob of the jar. Let the end of the other wire touch the ground.

When the circuit is complete, hundreds of little sparks will pass between the aluminum foil squares, giving the appearance of lightning.

## Cylinder Electrical Machine

The cylinder electrical machine provides an alternative to the electrophorus, since it also provides electric charges. (See Figure 87.) The machine is a little difficult to make, however, and if you decide to try, you will need the help of someone who knows how to cut glass.

First you need a large glass bottle that is cylindrical in shape. If possible, get a bottle that is about 6 inches in diameter and 1 foot long; if not, get the largest bottle you can find.

Now if you know an adult who has had experience cutting glass, have him drill a hole in the center of the base of the bottle. Before he does so, you can build a little circular dam of putty around the spot on the bottom where the hole is to be drilled. Your helper will place the bottle, bottom side up, in a vise, and then pour enough oil into the dam to cool the drill as he drills through the glass. He should use an electric drill fitted with a corundum-tipped high-speed drill— the kind sold in craft shops and used to drill holes in china vases or glass bottles that are to be turned into lamps and thus are to be fitted with light cords.

When your helper has finished drilling the hole, remove the putty, and wash and dry the bottle.

Now you need a plastic rod that is 6 inches longer than the length of the bottle and a cork that fits into the mouth of the bottle. Insert the rod through the hole in the bottom of the bottle, pushing it through the bottle so that the end comes out through the mouth.

Drill a hole lengthwise through the center of the cork, making it large enough for you to insert the plastic rod. Put some PVA adhesive in the hole and insert the plastic rod, gluing it so that 3 inches of the rod stick out from the top of the cork.

When the glue is dry, glue the cork into the neck of the bottle, using wood glue. Glue the other end of the plastic rod into the hole in the bottle with epoxy resin. The rod should extend beyond the bottom of the bottle for 3 inches also.

Now make a wooden frame like the one shown in Figure 87, page 158. Using a piercing saw, cut the parts out of ½-inch-thick wood. Make the base 14 inches by 6 inches, and make two uprights, which will hold the bottle, 6 inches by 3 inches.

Make a crank handle for the bottle as shown in Figure 88c.

Drill a hole in one of the uprights, 1 inch from the top, making it large enough for you to insert and revolve the crank handle. Drill a hole in the other upright, making it large enough for the plastic rod that extends from the bottom of the bottle and placing it 1 inch from the top of the upright. Place the bottle, with its protruding rod, between the two uprights. Push the rod ends through the holes, then glue these two uprights to the base with wood glue.

Now you have to make a rubber, or a device for rubbing the cylindrical bottle. For the upright supporting the rubber, use a 1-inch-square wooden dowel that is 8 inches long. Take a piece of chamois leather—the undressed leather used for window cleaning—and stuff it with kapok. Then tack the edges over the dowel, fastening them down with pins. The rubber is then screwed onto a separate stand. (See Figure 88b.)

Next you have to make a conductor. To do this, take a round wooden dowel 2 inches in diameter and 8 inches long and smooth it down with sandpaper. Drill a hole in the bottom end 1 inch deep making it wide enough to receive a plastic rod $\frac{1}{2}$ inch in diameter. Drill another hole in one end of the conductor to take the rod. The plastic rod must be 2 inches long, and a plastic bead $\frac{3}{4}$ inch across should be cemented to the end.

Another $\frac{1}{2}$ inch wooden rod supports the conductor. Its total length is 6 inches, but $\frac{1}{2}$ inch at each end is glued

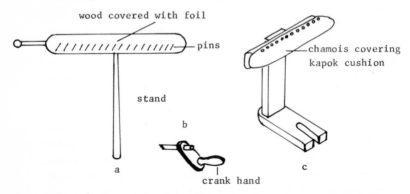

Figure 88. Prime conductor

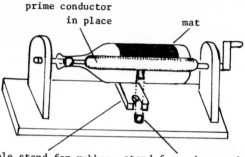

prime conductor
in place

mat

adjustable stand for rubber
screwed down on base

stand for prime conductor
Part of the conductor stand has
been cut away to show base of rubber.

Figure 89. Electrical machine with prime conductor and rubber in place.

into a hole drilled in the base and the bottom of the conductor.

Now make up the conductor as illustrated and attach it to the base of the machine. Using PVA adhesive, paste the whole surface of the conductor and knob and cover them with metal foil.

Cut the heads off twelve pins and push them into the side of the conductor, spacing them out as shown in the drawing. (Figure 88a.) Their points should be ¾ inch long and ¼ inch away from the cylinder.

Cut off the heads of the pins with a pair of pliers, and glue them into the conductor with wood glue. Mount the conducter on its rod, on the stand, on the opposite side of the bottle from the rubber.

Take a piece of silk varnished with shellac and tack it onto the rubber.

The machine is now complete. (See Figure 89.) When you turn the handle, the rubber will rub the cylinder and thus generate electricity, which will be collected by the pins in the conductor, and ½-inch sparks will be produced from the conductor. You will get the best results if you keep the machine clean and free of dust, warm it, and rub the bottle well with a warm woolen cloth.

# 10. Miscellaneous Toys

## The Cartesian Diver

When you made the barometers discussed in Chapter 7, you saw the effect of air pressure on water and mercury. The Cartesian diver is still another kind of pressure device.

Originally, the Cartesian diver was made from a hollow glass figure, but you can make one with any hollow figure, such as a plastic doll, since you might have trouble finding a glass one. A hollow plastic diver would be ideal, but if you can't find a diver, you can use some other kind of figure. Get a small figure, one that will fit into a tall glass jar, and get as tall a container as you can find. In addition, you need some lead shot, a piece of sheet rubber, such as a torn balloon or an old rubber kitchen glove, and some strong thread or string.

Fill the glass jar with water. Drill a hole in the bottom of the doll. Drop enough lead shot, made sticky with contact cement so that it will stay inside the doll, into the hole to make the doll float just below the surface of the water, and put the doll into the water. Then cover the top of the jar with the rubber, and tie it down firmly around the rim of the jar with the string.

When you press the rubber with your fingers, the doll will dive to the bottom of the jar, and when you remove your fingers, it will rise back to the surface. That is because the pressure of your fingers on the rubber increases the pressure on the water and thus forces water into the hole in the doll. As the water enters the doll, the doll loses its buoyancy and sinks. When you remove the pressure by lifting your fingers, the water flows back out of the doll, and as the doll regains its buoyancy, it rises toward the surface.

### The *Pantin*

A popular French toy in the eighteenth century, the *pantin* is a figure with movable arms and legs, which can be manipulated with pull strings. An example is shown in Figure 90. You can buy expensive versions of this toy today, but you can also make yourself one at very little cost.

To do so, first draw the figure's body and head, arms, and legs, using Figure 91 as a guide, on a piece of hardboard. Make the body and head 6¼ inches tall, and make the body 2¼ inches wide. Make the upper part of the leg 2¼ inches long and the bottom part 2¼ inches long. Make the whole arm 3 inches long. Then cut the parts out with a fretsaw and smooth down the rough edges with sandpaper.

Drill a hole ⅛ inch in diameter in each of the arms and

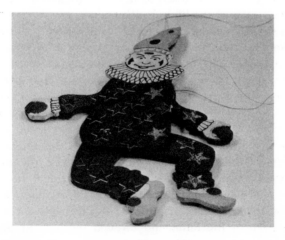

Figure 90. The *pantin*

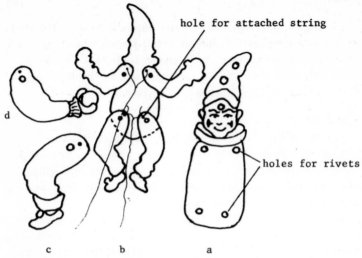

hole for attached string

holes for rivets

d

c          b          a

Figure 91. Parts for the *pantin*
(a) body; (b) assembled *pantin* from the back; (c) leg; (d) arm.

legs, placing the hole ¼ inch from the top of the limb. Drill
four more holes, also ⅛ inch in diameter, in the body where
the limbs are to be attached to it. All of these holes are rivet
holes for attaching the limbs to the body.

Drill slightly smaller holes for the pull strings. Drill one of
these holes at the top of each limb, placing it ⅛ inch above
the rivet holes, and one in the top of the *pantin's* hat.

Now you can paint the parts of the *pantin*. First give them
a coat of priming paint, then use plastic paint—the kind used
to paint miniature soldiers (Humbrol enamel)—to paint the
clothing and the face. Thin some paint with paint thinner
and use that, applying it with a pen, to paint the facial details.
You can use self-adhesive gilt stars to decorate the *pantin's*
clown costume and colored roundels to ornament his hat.

When you have finished painting the figure, insert a piece
of strong nylon thread, 12 inches long, through the smaller
hole in each of the limbs and through the hole in the hat,

and tie a knot in the end of the threads. Now put the parts together. To do this, lay one of the limbs on top of the body so that the appropriate rivet holes are aligned. Put a rivet, $\frac{1}{8}$ inch wide and $\frac{1}{4}$ inch long, through the two holes from the front of the figure, and open it up at the back. Attach the other limbs in the same way, making sure the rivets are not too tight and the limbs can move freely.

Spread the *pantin* out, face downward. Take the two threads that are tied to the arms and tie them together, about $\frac{1}{2}$ inch from the ends attached to the arms. Then cut one of the threads off above the knot tying the two together. Do the same with the two threads attached to the legs.

Hold the *pantin* by the thread attached to the top of the hat, and when you pull the strings attached to the arms and legs, the limbs should immediately spring to life. If they are sluggish when they move up and down, put small weights

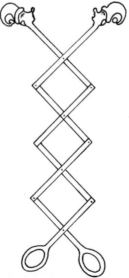

Figure 92. Scissors toy

behind the hands and feet, gluing them on with impact adhesive.

## The Scissors Toy

The scissors toy, shown in Figure 92, is a great favorite with young children. You can amuse a younger brother or sister by crouching behind a bed and working the toy so the two heads on it suddenly appear above the bed or by operating it so the heads appear from around a corner.

To make a scissors toy, cut four strips of wood, 1 inch wide, out of $\frac{1}{2}$-inch-thick wood. The strips for the middle of the toy should be 17 inches long, those at the ends, 21 inches long. Cut out two more strips, each with the loop of a scissors handle at the end. (See Figure 92.) Draw these strips on the wood before attempting to cut them out. Use a coping saw or piercing saw to cut out the loops.

Finally, cut out two more strips, 1 inch wide. These are the strips to which you will attach the two heads. You can draw the heads on $\frac{1}{2}$-inch-thick wood, cut them out with a coping saw, and glue them to the ends of the strips with wood glue. Or if you prefer, you can get two cheap dolls, remove their heads, and fasten the heads to the ends of the strips. As an added attraction, you can put fabric caps with bells on the ends, like those in Figure 92, on the heads.

If you decide to use dolls' heads, you will probably find it easier to put the rest of the toy together before attaching the heads. If you want to cut the heads out of wood, however, you can do that now.

Then take all the wooden parts, including the two wooden heads if that is what you are using, smooth them down with sandpaper and paint them with a coat of primer. When the paint is dry, you can glue the two wooden heads to the ends of the strips for them.

Now drill holes for rivets, making them $\frac{1}{8}$ inch in diameter. Make a hole at both ends of the four strips that do not have handles or heads, placing the holes ½ inch from the end. Drill another hole in the center of these strips. In the strips that will form the scissors handle, drill a hole at the end opposite the loop, also placing the hole ½ inch from the end. In the strips for the heads drill a hole in the end opposite the head and another hole ½ inch from that end.

When the rivet holes are done, you can finish painting the toy. Paint the different strips of wood in contrasting colors, and if you have used wooden heads, paint on the facial features.

Now to assemble the parts. Lay two strips of wood over one another so that the holes overlap. Push a rivet right through the holes. Turn over the two pieces of wood. Open up the cleft of the rivet with a screwdriver. Hammer it gently so that it stays open.

Test the toy to make sure the rivets are not too tight by slipping your fingers into the loops and pressing the handle together. You should be able to open and close the trellis easily.

Once you have assembled the parts and they are operating properly, you can add the dolls' heads if that is what you have decided to use. To do this, glue them on with wood glue.

When the toy is finished, the heads will shoot out a considerable distance, so be careful not to get too close to someone, or the toy could hit him in the face.

### The Jack-in-the-Box

The jack-in-the-box is, of course, an all-time favorite with young children. To make a small one, like the one shown in Figure 93, take 4 feet of thin, springy wire and make it into a spring by winding it around a broom handle that is about an inch in diameter, keeping the rings of the wire close together. When you have wound it so it forms a spiral, slip the wire off the end of the broom handle. Cover the spring with a stitched muslin tube. In the drawing, the muslin is left off to show the construction.

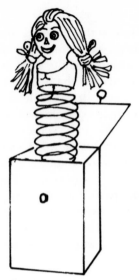

Figure 93. Jack-in-the-box

Next take a cork about 2 inches high, carve it so it is shaped like a head, and paint a face on it. You can cover the face with plastic paint and then put the eyes, nose, and mouth on top of that. To add hair, make a wig out of doll's hair or use some yellow or brown or black yarn. To make a wig of yarn, tie some yarn together in the middle with a single piece of yarn; tie ribbons around the ends, making bows, and glue the yarn to the top of the cork with contact cement.

When you have finished making the head, take an auger and make a hole in the center of the bottom of the cork. Then glue in the end of the spring, using wood glue.

Now to make the box for the toy. For this you need a cardboard box that is large enough to hold the figure and spring when compressed. If there is already a cover on the box, cut that off. Then make a lid out of a piece of stout cardboard, cutting the cardboard so it is the same size as the base of the box. Make a hinge for the lid by pasting a strip of fabric to the box and to the lid.

Take a piece of wire and make a loop at one end. Stick the other end into the front edge of the lid and glue it firmly into place. With an auger, make a hole in the front of the box, $1/2$ inch from the top. Cut the head off a plastic knitting needle and cement it into the hole. Decorate the outside of the box with contact paper or by pasting on some other kind of decorative paper.

Now make a hole in the bottom of the box with a bradawl. Slip the bottom end of the wire spring through the hole, and fasten it on the outside of the box by gluing a piece of fabric over it with PVA adhesive.

The jack-in-the-box is now complete. To make it work, press the head down into the box, and fasten the wire loop over the head of the knitting needle. Then slip the loop off, and the head will pop up suddenly.

6 K